THE CHRONICLES OF
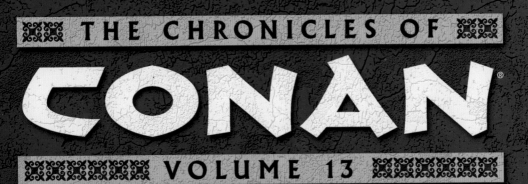

CONAN®

VOLUME 13

WHISPERING SHADOWS
AND OTHER STORIES

THE CHRONICLES OF

CONAN®

VOLUME 13

WHISPERING SHADOWS
AND OTHER STORIES

Based on the classic pulp
character **Conan the Barbarian,**
created by

ROBERT E. HOWARD

Written by

ROY THOMAS

Illustrated by

JOHN BUSCEMA,
SAL BUSCEMA
AND OTHERS

Coloring by

PETER DAWES, DONOVAN YACIUK
and **WIL GLASS** with **ALL THUMBS CREATIVE**

DARK HORSE BOOKS®

Publisher
MIKE RICHARDSON

Collection Designer
DARIN FABRICK

Art Director
LIA RIBACCHI

Collection Editor
MATT DRYER

Assistant Editor
RYAN JORGENSEN

Special thanks to Fredrik Malmberg, Leigh Stone and Dan Fierst at
Conan Properties; and to Roy Thomas.

This volume collects issues ninety-two, and one hundred and one through one hundred
and seven of the Marvel comic-book series **Conan the Barbarian**.

Published by Dark Horse Books
A division of Dark Horse Comics, Inc.
10956 SE Main Street
Milwaukie, OR 97222

www.darkhorse.com
www.conan.com

To find a comics shop in your area, call the Comic Shop Locator Service
toll-free at 1-888-266-4226

First edition: December 2007
ISBN 978-1-59307-837-9

3 5 7 9 10 8 6 4 2

Printed in China

TABLE OF CONTENTS

ALL STORIES WRITTEN BY ROY THOMAS

"Know, O prince, that between the years when the oceans drank Atlantis and the gleaming cities, and the rise of the sons of Aryas, there was an Age undreamed of, when shining kingdoms lay spread across the world like blue mantles beneath the stars. "Hither came Conan, the Cimmerian, black-haired, sullen-eyed, sword in hand, a thief, a reaver, a slayer, with gigantic melancholies and gigantic mirth, to tread the jeweled thrones of the Earth under his sandaled feet."

—*The Nemedian Chronicles.*

A TALE OF YOUNG CONAN™

THE THING IN THE CRYPT!

ADAPTED FROM THE STORY BY L. SPRAGUE DE CAMP & LIN CARTER

SPECIAL NEMEDIAN NOTE: WHILE BIG BROTHER *JOHN B.* WAS ENJOYING A BRIEF BUT WELL-EARNED VACATION IN FRANCE AND ITALY, OUR PAL *SAL BUSCEMA* STEPPED IN TO PENCIL THIS TALE OF CONAN'S EARLY DAYS. WE THINK IT'S JUST MILDLY *TERRIFIC*... AND, OH YES, FOR ALL YOU CHRONOLOGY BUFFS, THIS ISSUE'S STORY TAKES PLACE BETWEEN THE EVENTS RECORDED IN *ISSUES #2-3.* —R.T.

FOR TWO DAYS, THE *WOLVES* HAVE TRAILED HIM THROUGH THE WOODS... AND NOW, THEY ARE *CLOSING* IN ON HIM AGAIN...!

ROY THOMAS & **ERNIE CHAN**
WRITER / EDITOR   INKER / EMBELLISHER
welcome guest penciller
SAL BUSCEMA!

JOE ROSEN
LETTERER

JIM SHOOTER
CONSULTING EDITOR

FEATURING THE EPIC HERO CREATED BY **ROBERT E. HOWARD**

IN ORDINARY TIMES, AN ACTIVE MAN HAS **LITTLE TO FEAR** FROM WOLVES.

BUT, THIS IS THE **END** OF A LONG, COLD **WINTER**...

...AND THE **STARVING WOLVES** ARE READY FOR **ANY** DESPERATE CHANCE!

RRRRR

THEIR LEADER IS **NOT** PREPARED, HOWEVER, FOR A HUMAN WHO WIELDS A **CHAIN** WITH SUCH BANEFUL FURY AS **CONAN,** LATELY OF **CIMMERIA.**

BACK, YOU FANGED DEVIL!

THUS, WHEN THE WHITE, MELTING SNOW TURNS SUDDENLY **SCARLET**--

--THE FAMISHED **PACK** TURNS AWAY FROM THIS FIERCE-EYED LAD, TO FEAST INSTEAD UPON THEIR OWN **DEAD BROTHER.**

EVEN AS CONAN FLEES **SOUTHWARD,** HOWEVER, HE KNOWS THEY'LL SOON BE BACK UPON HIS **TRACK.**

8

ON HE RUNS, AS HE HAD DONE FOR **TWO DAYS** WITHOUT STOP... AND AS HE RUNS, HE **REMEMBERS**...

...**REMEMBERS** HOW, LEAVING HIS HOMELAND, HE WANDERED FIRST **NORTH**, NOT SOUTH...

...JOINING A BAND OF RAIDERS FROM **AESGAARD** WHO WERE HARRYING THE BORDERS OF SAVAGE **HYPERBOREA.**

A **NATURAL** ENOUGH THING FOR A **CIMMERIAN** TO DO...

...SINCE HIS PEOPLE HAVE EVER HAD A **BLOOD-FEUD** WITH THE HYPERBOREANS.

AT LENGTH, HE WAS **CAPTURED**... AND KNEW FOR THE FIRST TIME THE FEEL OF **CHAINS**...AND THE **LASH.**

HE DID **NOT**, HOWEVER, REMAIN **LONG** IN SLAVERY, BUT **WORKED AWAY** AT HIS HATED FETTERS...

...TILL ONE OF THE **LINKS** WAS WEAK ENOUGH FOR HIM TO **SNAP**, WITH AN EFFORT AT WHICH MOST MEN COULD ONLY **GASP.**

THEN, DURING A HEAVY RAINSTORM, HE **BURST FREE**, SLAYING HIS DESPISED HYPERBOREAN **OVER-SEER**--

--TO **VANISH** TO THE SENSES OF BOTH **MEN** AND **HOUNDS**, AMID THE DOWNPOUR.

NOW, AT **SUNSET**, HE KNOWS HE NEARS THE BOUNDARIES OF **BRYTHUNIA**...

YET, HIS CHANCES OF REACHING **SAFETY** THERE ARE FADING WITH EACH PASSING **SECOND**.

FOR, THE STILL-RAVENOUS **WOLVES** HAVE CAUGHT UP WITH HIM!

ARROOO

OUT ONTO THE SLUSHY ICE OF A **FROZEN RIVER** HE FLEES...

BUT, ANY FAINT **HOPE** HE HAD THAT THE WOLVES MIGHT **ABANDON** THEIR PURSUIT IS SWIFTLY **DISPELLED**.

HE **FIGHTS** THEM THERE ON THE SLIPPERY ICE, SWINGING HIS BLOODY **CHAIN** LIKE A FLAIL, KEEPING THE FEARSOME PACK AT **BAY**--

--TILL SUDDENLY, THE **BOLDEST** OF THE WOLVES **SEIZES** THE IRON LINKS BETWEEN **GRIM JAWS**.

LET GO, YOU--!

RRRR

NEXT MOMENT, EVEN AS THE CHAIN IS **TORN** FROM CONAN'S NUMB GRASP--

--THE **WEIGHT** OF WOLVES AND MEN **TELLS** UPON THE LATE-WINTER ICE--

UNNHH--!

--AND CONAN FINDS HIMSELF **GASPING** AND **CHOKING** IN THE ICY FLOOD!

HE KNOWS THAT **SEVERAL** OF THE WOLVES FELL IN **WITH** HIM, MOSTLY TO THEIR **DEATHS**...

STILL, AS HE HAULS HIMSELF **OUT** OF THE ICE ON THE **NETHER SIDE** OF THE RIVER...

...HE KNOWS THAT SEVERAL MORE **SURVIVED!**

DAMN YOUR SCRUFFY HIDES!

AND NOW-- HE IS **WEAPONLESS!**

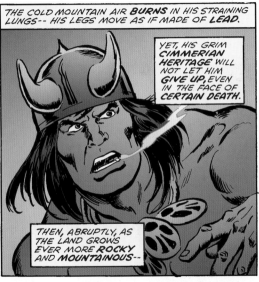

THE COLD MOUNTAIN AIR **BURNS** IN HIS STRAINING LUNGS-- HIS LEGS MOVE AS IF MADE OF **LEAD.**

YET, HIS GRIM **CIMMERIAN HERITAGE** WILL NOT LET HIM **GIVE UP,** EVEN IN THE FACE OF **CERTAIN DEATH.**

THEN, ABRUPTLY, AS THE LAND GROWS EVER MORE **ROCKY** AND **MOUNTAINOUS**--

--HE SEES A **YAWNING BLACKNESS** BETWEEN TWO **MIGHTY PLANES** OF ROCK.

A **CAVE!**

WITH NO THOUGHT OR FEAR OF WHAT MAY LIE **WITHIN,** HE HURLS HIMSELF **INTO** THE DARK CLEFT--

--AND **DROOLING JAWS** SNAP HARD ON **EMPTY AIR.**

RRR RRR

HE KNOWS THAT, A MOMENT MORE, AND THE WOLVES WILL BE *AFTER* HIM THROUGH THAT SELFSAME *CLEFT*...

THUS, HE SEARCHES ABOUT, FRANTICALLY, FOR SOMETHING-- *ANYTHING*-- TO USE AS A *WEAPON* AGAINST THE HOWLING HORDE.

HE FINDS... *NOTHING.*

YET, THOUGH THE PREDATORS *WHINE* OUTSIDE, HUNGRY FOR BLOOD, *NOT ONE* COMES THROUGH THE DIM, GRAY SLIT.

AND THAT IS *STRANGE.*

LOOKING ABOUT AS BEST HE *CAN* IN THE NIGH-UTTER BLACKNESS, CONAN CAN TELL HE IS IN A *NARROW CHAMBER* IN THE ROCK... ITS UNEVEN FLOOR STREWN WITH THE *LITTER* BLOWN IN BY CENTURIES OF UNCARING *WIND.*

WITH OUT-STRETCHED HAND, HE BEGINS TO *EXPLORE* AS BEST HE *CAN.*

SOON, HE COMES UPON ANOTHER, *SMALLER* DOOR-WAY, AND--

HUH--?

HIS QUESTING FINGERS AND STRAINING EYES TELL HIM THERE ARE *CHISEL MARKS* ON THE STONE...

...FORMING CRYPTIC *GLYPHS* OF SOME UNKNOWN *WRITING!*

UNKNOWN, AT LEAST, TO THE *UNTUTORED CIMMERIAN YOUTH,* FRESH FROM ILLITERATE VILLAGES.

AS HE *STOOPS* TO ENTER THE INNER DOORWAY, HE WONDERS UNEASILY WHO *CARVED* SUCH A DOORWAY HERE...

...AND *WHY.*

STANDING UP WITHIN, HE **LISTENS** WARILY.

THOUGH THE **SILENCE** IS ABSOLUTE, SOME **SIXTH SENSE** SEEMS TO WARN HIM THAT HE IS **NOT ALONE** IN THE CHAMBER.

IN **TOTAL DARKNESS** NOW, HIS SHUFFLING FEET ENCOUNTER **OBJECTS** SCATTERED ABOUT THE FLOOR.

HE CANNOT **SEE** WHAT THEY ARE, BUT THEY DO NOT FEEL LIKE THE **FOREST LITTER** THAT CARPETED THE ANTECHAMBER.

THEY FEEL MORE LIKE... **MANMADE** THINGS.

THEN, AS HE TAKES A **QUICK STEP** ALONG THE WALL--

MMMFE--!

THE **SPLINTERING** SOUND TELLS HIM IT IS A **WOODEN** THING THAT HAS BROKEN BENEATH HIS WEIGHT...

...ADDING **ONE MORE SCRATCH** TO THOSE OF THE **WOLVES'** CLAWS.

CURSE ME FOR A CLUMSY **FOOL!**

AS FOR THAT ON WHICH HE **STUMBLED**--

--HE KNOWS ALMOST AT ONCE THAT IT WAS A **CHAIR**...

...COMPOSED OF **ROTTED WOOD.**

NOW, STILL AWARE OF THE **EERIE PRESENCE**, HE CONTINUES HIS EXPLORATIONS MORE **CAUTIOUSLY**...

THE **WHEELS** OF THE CHARIOT, HE PRESENTLY FINDS, HAVE **COLLAPSED** WITH THE ROTTING OF THEIR **SPOKES.**

THEN, CONAN'S QUESTING HANDS COME UPON SOMETHING COLD...*METALLIC.*

INSTANTLY, AN *IDEA* FORMS...

HE FINDS MORE BITS OF **WOOD** AND **STONE**...

...AND, AFTER SEVERAL FAILURES...

...HE SOON HAS A SMALL, SMOKY *FIRE* SPUTTERING.

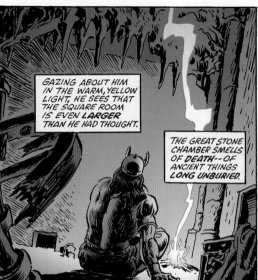

GAZING ABOUT HIM IN THE WARM, YELLOW LIGHT, HE SEES THAT THE SQUARE ROOM IS EVEN *LARGER* THAN HE HAD THOUGHT.

THE GREAT STONE CHAMBER SMELLS OF **DEATH**-- OF ANCIENT THINGS *LONG UNBURIED.*

AND THEN, THE *HAIR* LIFTS FROM THE NAPE OF HIS NECK, AS HE SENSES ONCE MORE... THE **PRESENCE** HE HAD NEARLY FORGOTTEN.

HE FIGHTS OFF THE *PARALYSIS* OF A NAMELESS, HALF-FORMED *FEAR,* TO TURN AND BEHOLD--

FOR A MOMENT, HE ALMOST FLEES BACK TOWARD THE *HUNGRY WOLVES*, RATHER THAN FACE THIS MONSTROUS, GRINNING *CADAVER...*

...IN WHOSE SUNKEN *SOCKETS* THE WAVERING FIRELIGHT SEEMS TO PAINT *DARK, BURNING* EYES.

THEN, STEELING HIMSELF, CONAN *DROPS* HIS GAZE TO--

--THE GREAT *SWORD* THAT LIES ACROSS THE CORPSE'S BONY *THIGHS!*

NOT LONG AGO, HE *TOSSED AWAY* A SWORD HE PULLED FROM A *STONE*, IN A HAUNTED CAVERN IN *VANAHEIM.**

HE HAS A NATURAL *AVERSION* TO ANYTHING THAT SMACKS OF *SORCERY...*

*SEE ISSUE #30.
-- R.T.

YET, THE *NOTCHES* IN THIS BLADE SPEAK OF BATTLES BETWEEN *MEN*-- EVEN IF IN A DISTANT, HALF-FABLED *PAST.*

PERHAPS *KING KULL* HIMSELF USED IT, IN *ATLANTEAN* DAYS, TO SLAY THE VENOMOUS *SERPENT-MEN* OF *VALUSIA!*

GODS! WHAT A *SWORD!*

WITH SUCH A SWORD, HE'LL *MORE THAN* HOLD HIS OWN WITH THE *STARVING* WOLVES THAT LURK WITHOUT!

EXPANDING HIS CHEST, THE LAD BOOMS OUT THE SAVAGE *WAR CRY* OF HIS FOLK--

--ITS ECHOES DISTURBING ANCIENT *SHADOWS* AND OLD *DUST.*

THEN, SUDDENLY-- A *SOUND...*

AN INDESCRIBABLE, DRY *CREAKING* FROM BEHIND HIM--

--AND HIS YOUNG BLOOD TURNS TO ICE IN HIS VEINS!

IT LIVES!!

THE CHALLENGE OF HIS EXUBERANT WAR CRY HAS BEEN ANSWERED-- BY A THING DEAD PERHAPS A THOUSAND CENTURIES!

BY WHAT PRIMEVAL MAGIC LIFE STILL ANIMATES THE WITHERED MUMMY OF SOME LONG-DEAD CHIEF, CONAN CANNOT GUESS.

YET, THAT SELF-SAME WIZARDRY HAS GIVEN VISION TO ITS EYELESS GAZE--

--AND DOUBT-LESS SUPER-HUMAN POWER TO ITS SHRIVELED, BROWNISH MUSCLES!

NOW, IT ADVANCES JERKILY TOWARD CONAN-- AND THE SWORD HE HOLDS...

17

NUMB WITH SUPERSTITIOUS HORROR, CONAN *RETREATS* STEP BY STEP AMID THE SHARDS AND SHADOWS OF THE ROOM.

SAVE FOR THE WEAK *CRACKLE OF FLAMES*-- THE RUSTLE OF THE CADAVER'S *LEATHERY MUSCLES* AGAINST ANCIENT *BONES*-- AND THE PANTING *BREATH OF THE YOUTH*--

--THE CHAMBER IS *SILENT AS A GRAVE!*

AT LENGTH, THE DEAD THING HAS *BACKED* CONAN AGAINST A *WALL.*

BUT, PERHAPS THAT IS WHAT *SAVES THE YOUTH*, FOR THE MOMENT--

FOR, CORNERED THUS, HE HAS NO RECOURSE BUT HIS OWN *INSTINCTS*--

--INSTINCTS WHICH TELL HIM TO *STRIKE*, BEFORE IT'S *TOO LATE!*

NO BLOOD SPURTS FROM THE SEVERED CLAW AS IT FALLS WITH A *DRY CLACK* TO THE FLOOR...

BUT NEITHER DOES THE WOUND *SLOW* THE WALKING CORPSE--

--AS IT EXTENDS ITS *OTHER* HAND-- TO LAY IT UPON THE TERRIFIED CIMMERIAN'S *SHOULDER!*

CROM HELP ME!

HE HAS NOT YET *LEARNED*--

CROM HELPS NO ONE--

DIE, YOU GRINNING SKELETON! **DIE!**

--WHO DOES NOT HELP **HIMSELF!**

BUT, EVEN AS THE CADAVER'S **RIBS** SNAP LIKE TWIGS BENEATH HIS SWORD--

--EVEN AS IT IS HURLED OFF ITS **FEET** WITH A CLATTER, TO SPRAWL ON THE ROCKY **FLOOR**--

--CONAN **REALIZES** AT LAST, WITH A GRIM **FINALITY**--

--THAT ONE **CANNOT** KILL--

--WHAT IS **ALREADY DEAD!**

AROUND AND AROUND THEY GO, **CIRCLING** SLOWLY-- AS **LEADEN ETERNITIES** DRAG BY.

THEN, ABRUPTLY-- A **BLOW** AT THE THING'S REMAINING **ARM**--

--WHICH MISSES ITS **MARK**--

--AND A SAVAGELY CLAWED **SHOULDER** REMINDS CONAN, IF REMINDER BE **NEEDED**--

UNNG

--THAT THIS IS THE **MOST REAL** OF **NIGHTMARES!**

NOTHING, IT SEEMS, CAN STOP THIS GIGANTIC CREATURE WHICH WAS ONCE A PRIMITIVE KING--

--NOTHING--

--NOT EVEN A BLOW TO ITS DRY, BROWNISH SKULL!

THE BLADE STICKS THERE FOR AN INSTANT--

--AN INSTANT THAT NEARLY MEANS THE YOUNG BARBARIAN'S OWN DEATH!

ARRR

HEAD-- ARM-- EVEN RIBS AND SPINE:

CONAN HAS TRIED THEM ALL NOW, IN HIS EXTREME DESPERATION...

NOTHING CAN STOP IT...OR EVEN HURT IT.

AND THE YOUTH IS TIRING FAST NOW, AS ONCE MORE THE QUESTION ECHOES MADLY IN HIS BRAIN--

HOW CAN YOU KILL A THING THAT IS ALREADY DEAD?

ROUND AND ROUND THE QUESTION GOES IN HIS HEAD...TILL HE THINKS HE WILL GO MAD.

20

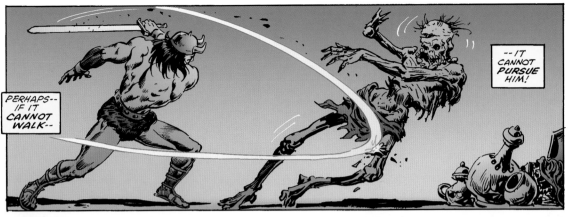

PERHAPS-- IF IT *CANNOT WALK*--

--IT *CANNOT PURSUE* HIM!

YET, IT STAGGERS LURCHINGLY TO ITS *FEET*--

--DRAGGING ITS CRIPPLED LEG BEHIND IT.

AGAIN CONAN STRIKES-- *DESPAIR* RISING WITHIN HIM NOW--

--AS HE *SHEARS AWAY* THE DEAD THING'S *LOWER FACE!*

ITS *JAW-BONE* GOES RATTLING OFF INTO *SHADOWS--*

BUT THE CORPSE-KING *NEVER STOPS!*

THEN-- *SOMETHING* CATCHES THE YOUTH'S *ANKLE*, PULLING HIM OFF-BALANCE ONTO THE CAVERN *FLOOR...*

WHAT THE *DEVIL*--?

...AND HIS BLOOD FREEZES *ANEW* AS HE BEHOLDS THE *SEVERED HAND* OF THE CADAVER *CLUTCHING* HIS FOOT--

--ITS *BONY CLAWS* BITING INTO HIS *FLESH!*

UNNNHH--!

NEXT MOMENT, A *GRISLY SHAPE* LOOMS OVER HIM--

--ITS *TALONED* HAND DARTING TOWARD HIS *THROAT!*

ONCE AGAIN, HE REACTS BY SHEER *INSTINCT*--

--AND WITH A *GOOD FORTUNE* WHICH MIGHT HAVE BEEN CAUSED BY THE *GODS' OWN SMILE.*

HERE, HAND! YOU *BELONG* WITH YOUR *MASTER*--

--SO TO *FLAMING HELL* WITH BOTH OF YOU!!

TURNING, THE YOUTH SNATCHES UP HIS PURLOINED *SWORD* AGAIN--

--ONLY TO FIND THE BATTLE ENDED!

DESICCATED BY LONG CENTURIES, THE MUMMY *BURNS* WITH THE FIERCE FURY OF *DRY BRUSHWOOD*...

...THOUGH IT STILL *STRUGGLES* TO ITS *FEET.*

IT HAS ALMOST CLAMBERED **OUT** OF THE NOW-RAGING **FIRE**...

...WHEN ITS **SHATTERED LEG** GIVES WAY!

WITHIN MINUTES, THE CADAVER IS UTTERLY **CONSUMED**, BUT FOR A FEW GLOWING COALS OF **BLACKENED BONE**.

THE MUMMY IS AT LAST **TRULY DEAD**...

...AND THE **GREAT SWORD** IS HIS!

NOW, **REVULSION** SEIZES THE YOUTH-- FOR, THE SMOKE-FILLED CHAMBER STINKS OF THE BURNING OF **LONG-DEAD HUMAN FLESH**--

--AND THE EMPTY THRONE SEEMS TO **LEER** AT HIM.

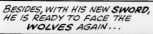

HIS **SCALP** CRAWLS AND HIS **SKIN** PRICKLES, AT THE THOUGHT OF **SLEEPING** IN THIS HAUNTED PLACE.

BESIDES, WITH HIS NEW **SWORD**, HE IS READY TO FACE THE **WOLVES** AGAIN...

...THOUGH, EMERGING FROM THE CAVE, HE FINDS **NO SIGN** OF THEM.

A GLANCE UP-WARD SHOWS THAT THE **SKY** IS CLEARING.

CONAN STUDIES FOR A MOMENT THE **STARS** THAT GLIMMER BETWEEN PATCHES OF **CLOUD**...

...THEN, ONCE MORE SETS HIS FOOT-STEPS TO **SOUTHWARD**.

NEMEDIAN CHRONICLERS' NOTE: WE KNOW, OF COURSE, THAT YOUNG CONAN **LOST** HIS STRANGE IF UNMAGICAL SWORD ERE LONG, WHEN HE WAS CAPTURED BY A **SECOND** GROUP OF WARLIKE **HYPERBOREANS**, NOT FAR FROM THE BORDERS OF **BRYTHUNIA**. AND PERHAPS, IN HIS WAY, THE CIMMERIAN WAS **LUCKY**, AT THAT-- FOR CAN ANY **GOOD THING** COME OUT OF A **CRYPT**--?

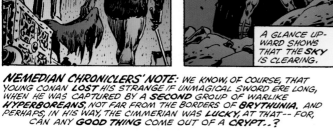

NEXT ISSUE: **AT LAST! REVENGE AT ASGALUN!**

"Know, O prince, that between the years when the oceans drank Atlantis and the gleaming cities, and the rise of the sons of Aryas, there was an Age undreamed of, when shining kingdoms lay spread across the world like blue mantles beneath the stars.
"Hither came Conan, the Cimmerian, black-haired, sullen-eyed, sword in hand, a thief, a reaver, a slayer, with gigantic melancholies and gigantic mirth, to tread the jeweled thrones of the Earth under his sandaled feet."

—*The Nemedian Chronicles.*

Stan Lee PRESENTS: CONAN THE BARBARIAN®

THE DEVIL HAS MANY LEGS!

FIRE! SMALL WONDER IT HAS BEEN WORSHIPPED AS A CRIMSON DEITY IN COUNTLESS PLACES, MYRIAD TIMES.

IT CAN WARM COLD BONES... KEEP WILD BEASTS AT BAY... AND MAKE AN ANTELOPE STEAK FAR MORE PALATABLE.

THIS NIGHT, HOWEVER, CONAN SEES IN THOSE NIGHT-LICKING FLAMES ONLY GHOSTLY SHADOWS OF A *CORSAIR SHIP,* BURNING AS SHE DRIFTS SLOWLY OUT INTO A MORNING SEA.

BÊLIT...

ROY THOMAS
WRITER/EDITOR

JOHN BUSCEMA & ERNIE CHAN
ILLUSTRATORS

JOE ROSEN
LETTERER

JIM SHOOTER
CONSULTING EDITOR

FEATURING THE EPIC HERO CREATED BY **ROBERT E. HOWARD**

LG-454

IT IS NOT, HOWEVER, THE SOUND OF CONAN'S OWN HALF-SPOKEN WORD THAT COMES ECHOING SOFTLY BACK TO HIM...

...BUT THE FAINT NOISE OF A *TWIG* SNAPPING, SOMEWHERE JUST BEYOND THE HALO OF LIGHT.

SOME FOUR-PAWED, NIGHT-PROWLING *PREDATOR*, OR...

...MAN!

NO MORE TIME NOW FOR THOUGHTS OF LOVE'S SAD LOSS, AS A VERY REAL *ARROW* THWANGS INTO THE LOG ON WHICH HE SITS--

--BUT ONLY OF *LIFE'S PRE-SERVATION.*

FOR THE FIRST TIME, HE IS *GLAD* HIS TORN CLOAK IS STILL SOGGY FROM THE AFTERNOON SHOWERS.

SMOKE WILL SHIELD HIS MOVEMENTS, EVEN AS THE FIRE DROWNS.

THEN, A BID FOR *FREEDOM*, IN THE OPPOSITE DIRECTION FROM WHENCE CAME THE SHAFT, BUT--!

THE FIGURE WHICH CROUCHES BEFORE HIM, SPEAR IN HAND, IS GRIMLY BRAVE...

...FOR ALL THE GOOD THAT DOES HIM AGAINST THE CIMMERIAN'S THIRSTY SWORD!

AAIEE

THEN, BENEATH THE JUNGLE HALF-MOON, THE DEATH-CRY IS ANSWERED--

EEYAA

--BY A *DOZEN* SAVAGE THROATS!

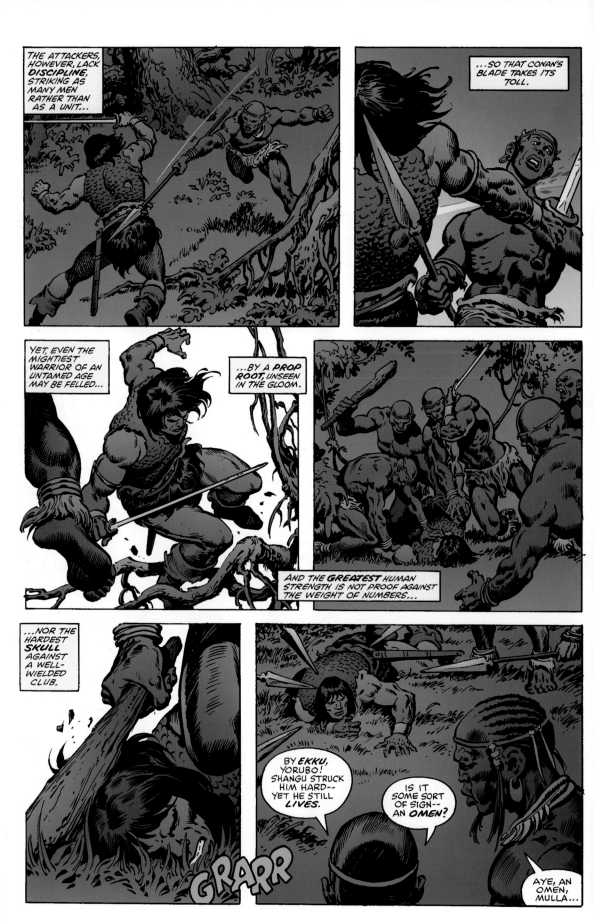

THE ATTACKERS, HOWEVER, LACK *DISCIPLINE,* STRIKING AS MANY MEN RATHER THAN AS A UNIT...

...SO THAT CONAN'S BLADE TAKES ITS TOLL.

YET, EVEN THE MIGHTIEST WARRIOR OF AN UNTAMED AGE MAY BE FELLED...

...BY A *PROP ROOT,* UNSEEN IN THE GLOOM.

AND THE *GREATEST* HUMAN STRENGTH IS NOT PROOF AGAINST THE WEIGHT OF NUMBERS...

...NOR THE HARDEST *SKULL* AGAINST A WELL-WIELDED CLUB.

GRARR

BY *EKKU,* YORUBO! SHANGU STRUCK HIM HARD-- YET HE STILL *LIVES.*

IS IT SOME SORT OF SIGN-- AN *OMEN?*

AYE, AN OMEN, MULLA...

...AN OMEN THAT HE SHOULD BE SKEWERED WITH A *SPEAR* HE'LL CARRY WITH HIM TO THE *WORLD BENEATH THE WORLD!*

HOLD! IT IS TRUE THAT THE BRONZE ONE'S FIRST SWORD-THRUST KILLED OUR *WAR-CHIEF...*

STILL, IT IS NOT FOR *YOU* TO ASSUME THAT ROLE, WITHOUT THE HOLDING OF A *TRIBAL COUNCIL.*

MULLA SPEAKS *TRUTH!* UNTIL THEN, THE CAPTIVE SHOULD *LIVE.*

IF THAT IS THE *WILL OF THE BAMULAS*, THEN IT IS THE WILL ALSO OF *YORUBO.*

WE SHALL TAKE THE WHITE DOG BACK TO OUR *VILLAGE...*

BUT FIRST, *BIND* HIM WELL-- AND REMOVE THE *METAL ROBE* THAT PROTECTS HIS CHEST!

IT IS AN OFFENSE UNTO *EKKU.*

THOUGH HIS DAYS WITH THE BLACK CORSAIRS HAVE TAUGHT HIM ENOUGH BLACK DIALECTS THAT HE *UNDERSTANDS* HIS CAPTORS' WORDS, CONAN GIVES NO OUTWARD SIGN...

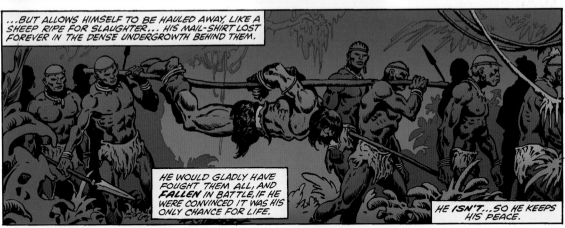

...BUT ALLOWS HIMSELF TO BE HAULED AWAY, LIKE A SHEEP RIPE FOR SLAUGHTER... HIS MAIL-SHIRT LOST FOREVER IN THE DENSE UNDERGROWTH BEHIND THEM.

HE WOULD GLADLY HAVE FOUGHT THEM ALL, AND *FALLEN* IN BATTLE, IF HE WERE CONVINCED IT WAS HIS ONLY CHANCE FOR LIFE.

HE *ISN'T*...SO HE KEEPS HIS PEACE.

THE ONE CALLED *YORUBO*, HOW- EVER, IS FAR FROM FINISHED WITH HIS BAITING...

I THINK YOU UNDERSTAND *MORE* THAT WE SAY THAN YOU PRETEND, JACKAL FROM THE NORTH.

NO MATTER! YOU UNDER- STAND THE LANGUAGE OF MY *SPEAR*, EH? *EH?*

THERE ARE MEN WHO, UPON MEETING FOR THE FIRST TIME, INSTANTLY RECOGNIZE EACH OTHER AS **NATURAL FOES**-- BORN ENEMIES WHOSE INESCAPABLE DESTINY IT IS TO **CLASH**, WHETHER THAT CLASH MAY COME AT ONCE, OR A LIFETIME LATER.

IN YORUBO, CONAN HAS RECOGNIZED JUST SUCH A FOE...

...AND THE BLACK WARRIOR HAS INSTINCTIVELY RETURNED THE FAVOR.

SOON, DOG, IT WILL BE JUST **YOU** AGAINST **ME**.

EKKU WILL BE ON **MY** SIDE, IN THAT HOUR.

ONLY CONAN'S SEARING EYES SPEAK FOR HIM.

IT IS A LONG DAY'S MARCH TO MORNING...AND TO THE INLAND VILLAGE OF THE FIERCE **BAMULA TRIBE**, OF WHICH CONAN HEARD EVEN WHEN HE WAS **AMRA**, SCOURGE OF THE BLACK COAST.

THEIR VILLAGE IS NOT LARGE BY THE STANDARDS OF THE HYBORIAN CITIES...BUT HE SEES AT ONCE THEY ARE A FAR MORE **POWERFUL** TRIBE THAN MOST HE HAS ENCOUNTERED IN THE BLACK LANDS.

AND PRESIDING OVER ALL IS THE KUSHITE GOD **EKKU**-- GRIM DEITY OF BLIND **CHANCE**-- CARVED HERE FROM WOOD, YET BURNED WITH AN IRON BRAND FOREVER INTO THE MINDS AND HEARTS OF THE BAMULAS.

N'YAGA, LATE SHAMAN OF THE BLACK CORSAIRS, ONCE TOLD HIM SOMETHING OF IMPORTANCE ABOUT EKKU AND HIS WAYS.

IT WAS SOMETHING **IMPORTANT**, YET TRY AS HE MIGHT, CONAN CANNOT QUITE--

JUST THEN, HE SPIES AGAIN THE HATED **YORUBO**... AND MUST BLINK HIS EYES TO BE CERTAIN IT IS INDEED YORUBO HE SEES FROM AFAR.

FOR, THE DARK EYES THAT STARE INTO THE WARRIOR'S ARE FILLED WITH **LOVE**... ADMIRATION...

...FEELINGS CONAN WOULD NOT HAVE BELIEVED YORUBO COULD INSPIRE, EVEN IN A **WIFE**.

THE CIMMERIAN IS YOUNG YET, AND STILL HAS MUCH TO LEARN.

SOON, SECURED AGAINST A THICK POLE WITH STRONG BONDS, HE FINDS HIMSELF LEFT **ALONE** TO BROOD...

...ALONE, THAT IS, SAVE FOR THE TAUNTINGS OF **CHILDREN**, WHOSE NATURAL CRUELTY HAS NOT YET BEEN TEMPERED BY THE COMPROMISES OF ADULTHOOD.

NIGHT COMES AGAIN, IF SLOWLY-- AND WITH IT, A **RITUAL** MOST OMINOUS--

A LITHE WARRIOR--OBVIOUSLY AN EARLIER **CAPTIVE**-- IS BROUGHT FORTH FROM A COMPOUND, AMID MUCH SPEAR-WAVING AND UNINTELLIGIBLE CHANTING TO **EKKU**--

--AND TOSSED INTO A **PIT** IN THE MIDST OF THE VILLAGE.

AAAA

SOMEHOW, CONAN IS NOT SURPRISED WHEN THE VICTIM'S **SCREAMS** DO NOT LONG ENDURE.

HE DOES NOT PRECISELY RECOGNIZE THE EERIE **SOUNDS** WHICH ISSUE THEN FROM THE PIT, OVER WHICH **THICK WOODEN BARS** ARE SWIFTLY REPLACED...

BUT, HE KNOWS THE **LOOK** IN THE EYES OF YORUBO'S WIFE, AS SHE SHRINKS FROM THE SCENE.

SHE SEEMS UNDULY SENSITIVE...FOR A BAMULA.

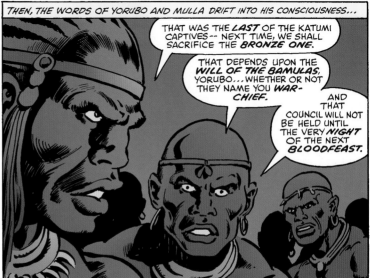

THEN, THE WORDS OF YORUBO AND MULLA DRIFT INTO HIS CONSCIOUSNESS...

THAT WAS THE **LAST** OF THE KATUMI CAPTIVES-- NEXT TIME, WE SHALL SACRIFICE THE **BRONZE ONE**.

THAT DEPENDS UPON THE **WILL OF THE BAMULAS**, YORUBO...WHETHER OR NOT THEY NAME YOU **WAR-CHIEF**.

AND THAT COUNCIL WILL NOT BE HELD UNTIL THE VERY **NIGHT** OF THE NEXT **BLOODFEAST**.

THE NEXT SEVERAL DAYS PASS LIKE A *NIGHTMARE,* WHETHER SUN SHINES OR WAXING MOON... BUT CONAN STOICALLY KEEPS HIS GRIM SILENCE...

...THOUGH WORKING ALL THE WHILE AT HIS *WRIST-BONDS* WITH A STRENGTH AND DETERMINATION AT WHICH EVEN THE BAMULAS DO NOT GUESS.

THEN, ON A NIGHT FULL OF *MOON...*

BRING THE *BRONZE ONE* ALONG, BUT KEEP HIS WRISTS BOUND!

AYE, MULLA.

THE EXPECTED TROUBLE IS NOT LONG IN COMING...

MULLA-- WHAT DO YOU WITH THE CAPTIVE?

HE IS TO BE SACRIFICED TO THE *MANY-LEGGED ONE* THIS NIGHT... AFTER I AM DECLARED *WAR-CHIEF!*

IF YOU ARE, YORUBO!

UNTIL THAT TIME, HE IS IN *MY* CHARGE, AND I SAY HE COMES WITH--

BY THE TWO FACES OF *EKKU*--

--I'VE WASTED WORDS *ENOUGH!*

AA!!!

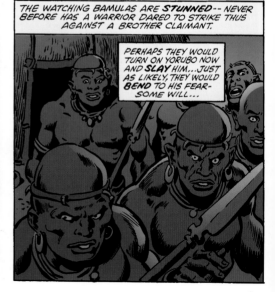

THE WATCHING BAMULAS ARE *STUNNED*-- NEVER BEFORE HAS A WARRIOR DARED TO STRIKE THUS AGAINST A BROTHER CLAIMANT.

PERHAPS THEY WOULD TURN ON YORUBO NOW AND *SLAY* HIM... JUST AS LIKELY, THEY WOULD *BEND* TO HIS FEARSOME WILL...

CONAN, HOWEVER, PREFERS **ACTION** TO THE WAITING GAME...

MEN OF THE BAMULAS-- I **CHALLENGE** YORUBO--

--IN THE NAME OF THE GREAT GOD **EKKU!**

SO, YOU **DO** UNDERSTAND! THEN LET YOUR **FIRST** BAMULA WORDS BE YOUR LAST--!

HOLD, YORUBO! HE SPOKE THE NAME OF **EKKU,** GOD OF FORTUNE!

HEAR HIM OUT!

YOU SEE, YORUBO? YOUR BAMULA BROTHERS KNOW, AS I DO, THAT **ANY** MAN-- EVEN A CAPTIVE-- MAY CHALLENGE ONE WHO CLAIMS THE **WAR-CHIEF'S SPEAR.**

AND SO THEY HAVE GIVEN **YOU** A SPEAR, EH?

IS THIS, THEN, THE **WILL OF THE BAMULAS?**

IN THE ENSUING CLAMOR, THE VOICES OF THE FOLLOWERS OF DEAD **MULLA** ARE THE LOUDEST...

AYE, YORUBO! FIGHT THE BRONZE ONE!

LET **EKKU** DECIDE WHO LIVES-- AND WHO DIES!

LET IT BE SO!

THE RITUAL, NO DOUBT, HAS BEEN ENACTED COUNTLESS TIMES IN THE PAST:

THE MASSIVE WOODEN BARS ARE REMOVED FROM OVER THE NEARBY PIT, A SINGLE GREAT **LOG** PLACED ACROSS IT...

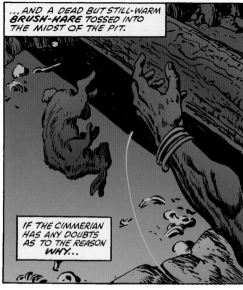

...AND A DEAD BUT STILL-WARM **BRUSH-HARE** TOSSED INTO THE MIDST OF THE PIT.

IF THE CIMMERIAN HAS ANY DOUBTS AS TO THE REASON **WHY...**

...THEY ARE SWIFTLY *DISPELLED.*

NEVER, SAVE IN THE ZAMORIAN CITY OF **YEZUD, THE SPIDER-GOD,** * HAS CONAN EVER BEHELD AN ARACHNID LARGER, MORE MONSTROUS...AND, THOUGH THIS VENOM-DRIPPING CREATURE IS FAR SMALLER THAN HUGE **OMM,** AND SCARCELY THE SIZE OF TWO LARGE MEN...

...'TIS ENOUGH... 'TWILL SERVE.

* CONAN #13. --R.T.

FROM SUBTERRANEAN CAVERNS AND TUNNELS DOES THE MANY-LEGGED ONE COME, DRAWN AS EVER BY THE **SCENT OF BLOOD**...

THIS NIGHT, HOWEVER, THE BLOOD-SMELL THAT DREW HIM HITHER IS FROM A BEAST FAR TOO **SMALL** TO SATE HIS BOTTOMLESS APPETITE.

STILL, THERE IS THE SCENT OF **OTHER** WARMBLOODS AROUND...AND THE NIGHT IS YOUNG.

YORUBO-- **NO!** *I HAVE SEEN YOUR HEART SWELL WHEN YOU HAVE DREAMED OF BECOMING WAR-CHIEF OF THE BAMULAS--*

BUT **THIS**--! IF YOU **FALL,** MY HUSBAND--!

THEN YOU WILL HAVE MY **SLAYER** AS YOUR MATE.

NOW **GET BACK,** WOMAN--

ONLY **MEN** CAN KNOW WHAT MUST BE DONE THIS NIGHT!

CONAN DOES NOT DEIGN TO ANSWER...FOR, GIVEN A CHOICE, HE WOULD FLEE LIKE THE VERY **DEVIL** FROM THIS VILLAGE, RATHER THAN FACE THE NIGH-MINDLESS **THING** CLACKING HUNGRILY BELOW.

BUT, HE HAS **NO** CHOICE... FOR, A HUNDRED BAMULA SPEARS WOULD CUT HIM DOWN IF HE TRIED TO ESCAPE.

THUS, WITH WIDELY DIFFERING MOTIVES-- OF **POWER,** AND OF MERE **SURVIVAL**-- THE TWO POWERFULLY BUILT WARRIORS EDGE OUT TOWARD THE MIDDLE OF THE HUGE ROUGH-BARKED LOG.

32

PERHAPS YORUBO HAS *PRACTICED*, IN SECRET, FOR THIS NIGHT.

UNNH

AT ANY RATE, IT IS *HE* WHO STRIKES FIRST, WITH PAINFUL SPEAR-HAFT--

--FOLLOWING UP THAT BLOW WITH *ANOTHER*, WHICH NEARLY CRACKS HIS PALER-SKINNED FOE'S RIBS--

AND THE WOMAN WHO LOVES *HIM* IS FEARFUL FOR HER MATE'S *LIFE* IF HE LOSES...

...FOR HIS *SOUL* IF HE WINS.

--WHILE *JET-BLACK HORROR* WAITS BELOW, UNABLE TO LEAP *QUITE* HIGH ENOUGH.

AS FOR *CONAN*-- HE HAS FOUGHT IN MANY A STRANGE ARENA, BUT NONE MORE WONDROUSLY WEIRD, MORE DANGEROUSLY DEADLY, THAN THIS.

HE IS GETTING THE *HANG* OF IT NOW, THIS FIGHTING WITH HAFTS OF SPEARS... AND GIVEN A BIT OF TIME, MIGHT EVEN TRIUMPH.

YORUBO, HOWEVER, DOESN'T *GIVE* HIM THAT TIME...

HNNNRH--!

ANOTHER MAN WOULD DOUBTLESS TOPPLE *FROM* THE LOG.

FROM BIRTH, HOWEVER, THE HILLMEN OF CIMMERIA POSSESS *UNCANNY* BALANCE...

...AND HE *SQUIRMS* DESPERATELY ON THE LOG, STRIVING TO REGAIN HIS EQUILIBRIUM, EVEN FALLEN ON HIS BACK.

EKKU *CANNOT* WILL IT THAT YOU DEFEAT ME, BRONZE DOG.

HE *CANNOT!*

HAVING USED THE KUSHITE GOD OF CHANCE TO FORCE YORUBO INTO THIS CLASH, CONAN HAS LITTLE MORE *USE* FOR WHAT EKKU WILLS OR DOES NOT WILL...

AARRH!

...THOUGH, TO THE WIDE-EYED WATCHING BAMULAS, QUITE THE *OPPOSITE* MUST SEEM TRUE.

YET, PERHAPS EKKU IS **NOT** BLIND TO HIS WORSHIPPERS, AFTER ALL...

FOR, THROUGH A QUIRK OF FATE, THE WARRIOR LANDS WITH FULL FORCE UPON THE HUGE SPIDER'S **BACK!**

YORUBO, MY HUSBAND-- I COME!

I SHALL **SAVE** YOU WITH THE **DAGGER OF MY FATHER**--

--OR ELSE WE DIE **TOGETHER**, IN THE GODS' ARMS!

UNTIL THIS MOMENT, CONAN'S PATH WAS CLEAR--

PROCLAIM HIMSELF THE **NEW WAR-CHIEF**, AND LET YORUBO FEND FOR HIMSELF.

NOT FOR **HIM** IS A LATER DAY'S AFFECTED CONCERN FOR THE **FALLEN FOE.**

NOW, HOWEVER, AS THE GIANT ARACHNID TOSSES THE BAMULA FROM ITS HAIRY BACK AS A DUCK SHEDS WATER-- AND TURNS TOWARD BOTH **YORUBO** AND HIS COURAGEOUS **WIFE**--

--CONAN'S MIND IS MADE *FOR* HIM!

HYAAA!!

THE CIMMERIAN'S TRIBAL BATTLE-CRY STILL ECHOES THROUGH THE JUNGLE NIGHT AS HIS THIRSTY SPEAR DRINKS DEEP OF THE MONSTER'S STRANGE, THICK *ICHOR*--

YET, EVEN AS IT DOES, HE KNOWS THAT HE'S NOT STRUCK A *VITAL SPOT* THERE, AS HE MIGHT HAVE ON A LION OR WATER BUFFALO--

--A POINT BROUGHT SHUDDERINGLY HOME THE VERY NEXT *INSTANT!*

UNNH

THE SPIDER-THING IS *HURT*, YES-- HE CAN SEE THAT IN THE WAY IT TURNS MORE *SLOWLY* THIS TIME--

BUT STILL IT *TURNS*--

--AND CONAN WISHES TO CROM THAT HIS SPEAR-POINT WERE AS *POISON-LADEN* AS THE LETHAL JAWS OF THE NIGHTMARE CREATURE HE FACES!

HE KNOWS HE HAS BUT *ONE* THRUST LEFT IN HIM--

--SO HE MAKES IT *COUNT!*

THE SPEAR WOULD PASS DIRECTLY THROUGH THE SPIDER'S *BRAIN*-- IF IT HAD ONE, AS WE UNDERSTAND THE TERM--

AND CONAN, HOLDING THE *SLUGGISH* MONSTER AT BAY AS ITS MASSIVE, FURRY LEGS FLAP MADLY AGAINST HIM, *WORKS* HIS SPEAR AS HE MIGHT WORK A *LEVER*--

--TO TURN THE THING OVER ON ITS *BACK!*

H**A**H!

FOR A SEEMING EON, IT FLAILS ABOUT HELPLESSLY, ICHOR *FLOWING* NOW FROM *TWO* GAPING HOLES IN ITS LOATHSOME BODY--

--TILL AT LAST, THAT FLAILING GROWS MORE AND MORE *MECHANICAL*, AND THE BARBARIAN KNOWS THAT THE SPIDER IS IN ITS *DEATH-THROES.*

ALL THIS WHILE, TIME HAS *STOOD STILL* AS HE FOUGHT THERE IN THE SUNKEN ARENA...

AND IT IS ONLY THE *CRIES OF THE BAMULAS* FROM ABOVE THAT MAKE TIME BEGIN TO *FLOW* ONCE MORE--

HAIL THE BRONZE-SKIN!

LET US MAKE *HIM* OUR WAR-CHIEF!!

IN HIS OWN SAVAGE, INSTINCTIVE WAY, YORUBO IS EXPERIENCED IN THE PSYCHOLOGY OF THE MOB.

HE KNOWS HE HAS BUT AN *INSTANT* TO SLAY THE OUTSIDER AND STILL RETAIN THE FEAR AND RESPECT OF HIS TRIBE...

...AN INSTANT HE **SEIZES** BY THE THROAT!

YORUBO-- NO!!

ON SUCH THINGS, BEYOND ALL PREDICTING, ARE THE **DESTINIES OF NATIONS** POISED--

THE HALF-INVOLUNTARY CRY OF A **WOMAN**--

--PANTHERISH **REFLEXES**--

--AND **WRISTS** THAT SEEM AS STRONG AS IRON!

UNNNENH--!

A **SECOND** TABLEAU NOW, CARVED OF THE SAME TWO MIGHTY-SINEWED FIGURES--

THIS TIME, HOWEVER, BOTH THE AWED ONLOOKERS AND THE SILENT, STRAINING PROTAGONISTS SEEM TO KNOW HOW IT WILL END--

-- HOW IT **MUST** END--!

URRGG

FOR ALL HIS TREACHERY, YORUBO WAS A STRONG AND BOLD WARRIOR...

BUT THERE IS ONLY **ONE** CONAN OF CIMMERIA.

UHHHHHH..

ACROSS A LIFELESS CORPSE NOW, CONAN LOOKS AT YORUBO'S MATE, AND SHE AT HIM.

THERE IS SADNESS IN HIS EYES...

...AND IN HERS... **WHAT?**

THEN, UNSPEAKING, SHE TURNS AWAY...TO CLIMB THE ROPE PROFFERED IN STUNNED SILENCE BY THOSE ABOVE.

GRIM-EYED, CONAN PLAYS HIS **OWN** PART AS WELL...

...SO THAT, MOMENTS LATER...

HAIL CONAN-- WAR-CHIEF OF THE BAMULAS!

PRAISE BE TO EKKU, GOD OF FORTUNES!

HE NEEDS NO KNOWLEDGE OF THE BAMULA TONGUE TO INTERPRET THE NEXT ACTION:

YORUBO'S MATE IS **HIS** NOW... A **GIFT** OF EKKU...

AND SHE MOVES TOWARD HIM WITH KNEES UN- STEADY, EYES BRIMFUL OF TEARS HE WILL NOT UNDERSTAND FOR SOME YEARS YET.

WITH A SINGLE, EFFORTLESS GESTURE, HE PICKS UP THE FAINTING WOMAN...AND CARRIES HER OFF TOWARD THE WAR-CHIEF'S HUT.

LET THE WARRIORS BEHIND HIM THINK WHAT THEY WILL, AND MULL OVER THE NIGHT'S EVENTS FOR A TIME.

HIS PART OF IT, HE KNOWS, CAN ONLY **GROW** WITH EACH RE-TELLING...

...AND NONE CAN SEE THROUGH THATCHED WALLS.

WHAT'S YOUR NAME?

I AM FELIDA.

SLEEP, FELIDA.

WE WILL TALK TOMORROW.

HE KNOWS BETTER, EVEN IN HIS YOUTH, THAN TO TRY TO APOLOGIZE.

CONAN SLEEPS LIGHTLY, MOST TIMES... BUT TONIGHT, WORN OUT BY DEATH-STRUGGLES AFTER DAYS TIED TO A POST, HE SLEEPS **SOUNDLY**...

...SO SOUNDLY HE DOES NOT HEAR FELIDA WALK-ING STEALTHILY TO WHERE THE PREVIOUS WAR-CHIEF'S **KNIFE** HANGS IN ITS LEATHERN SHEATH.

HE DOES NOT HEAR THE SHORT, HALF-REPRESSED **SOBS** SHE UTTERS AS SHE LIFTS IT, BROWN HAND TREMBLING...

...OR THE **LONGER** ONE WHICH ESCAPES HER AS SHE DROPS THE UNBLOODIED WEAPON TO THE DUST-COVERED FLOOR OF THE HUT.

AND OUTSIDE, THE PALE MOON GOES DOWN AT LAST...

...TO MAKE WAY FOR A COPPER-COLORED SUN THAT WILL SET THE JUNGLE ABLAZE WITH LIGHT...!

NEXT ISSUE: **THE MEN WHO DRINK BLOOD!**

"Know, O prince, that between the years when the oceans drank Atlantis and the gleaming cities, and the rise of the sons of Aryas, there was an Age undreamed of, when shining kingdoms lay spread across the world like blue mantles beneath the stars.
"Hither came Conan, the Cimmerian, black-haired, sullen-eyed, sword in hand, a thief, a reaver, a slayer, with gigantic melancholies and gigantic mirth, to tread the jeweled thrones of the Earth under his sandaled feet."
—*The Nemedian Chronicles.*

Stan Lee Presents: CONAN THE BARBARIAN®

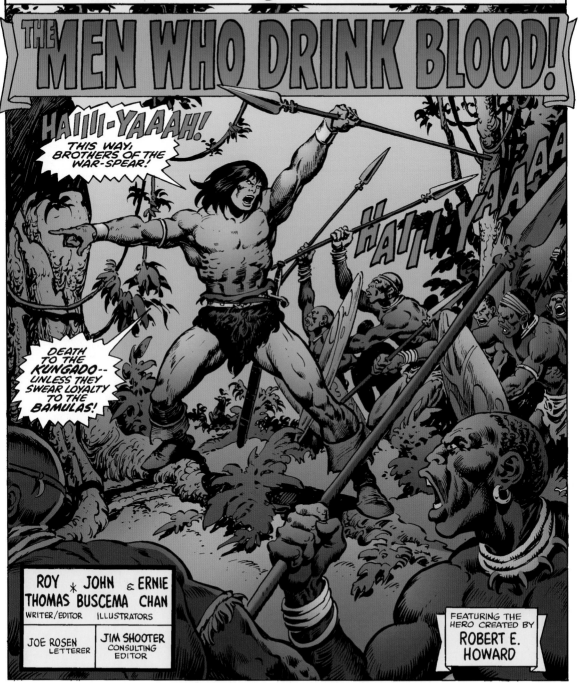

THE MEN WHO DRINK BLOOD!

HAIII-YAAAH!

THIS WAY, BROTHERS OF THE WAR-SPEAR!

DEATH TO THE KUNGADO-- UNLESS THEY SWEAR LOYALTY TO THE BAMULAS!

HAIIIYAAAA

ROY THOMAS
WRITER/EDITOR

JOHN BUSCEMA & ERNIE CHAN
ILLUSTRATORS

JOE ROSEN
LETTERER

JIM SHOOTER
CONSULTING EDITOR

FEATURING THE HERO CREATED BY ROBERT E. HOWARD

CONAN IS A *CIMMERIAN*-- BORN IN THE HIGH, WINDY HILLS OF A FAR-OFF LAND...

ARRRH

YET, SINCE SOON AFTER THE DEATH OF THE SHE-PIRATE BÊLIT, HE HAS BEEN PROUD TO BE *WAR-CHIEF* OF THE FIERCE *BAMULAS*--

THE *BAMULAS*-- BORN OF FIRE, AND SUCKLED ON THE BREASTS OF BATTLE--!

NOT LONG SINCE, THEY WERE A *FEARSOME* TRIBE--BUT STILL ONLY ONE OF *MANY*...

NOW, HOWEVER, CONAN IS FAST WIELDING THEM INTO THE HARBINGERS OF A FLEDGLING *EMPIRE*--

YYAAH

--AND ANY WHO WOULD *OPPOSE* THAT POWER WITH SPEAR OR ARROW OR LONG CURVED KNIFE--

--HAD BEST SEEK OUT THE AID OF *JUJU MAGIC*, AS WELL--

--IF HE'S TO STAND AGAINST THIS *MAN OF IRON*-- THESE THEWS OF NORTH-HEWN *STEEL!*

GRRXX

THIS BATTLE, LIKE A DOZEN OTHERS FOUGHT BY THE BAMULAS DURING THE PAST WEEKS, IS *OVER* ALMOST BEFORE IT HAS TRULY BEGUN...

HOLD, MEN OF THE BAMULAS! DO NOT SLAY US!

YOU HAVE KILLED OUR *CHIEF.*

WE THROW DOWN OUR SPEARS! *SPARE US!*

BAMULAS! HALT YOUR ATTACK!

I AM *CONAN*, WAR-CHIEF OF THE BAMULAS. WHO SPEAKS NOW FOR THE *KUNGADO?*

I, WHO AM *SON* TO HIM YOU SLEW.

YOU ARE A MIGHTY WARRIOR, AND WE OFFER YOU OUR ALLEGIANCE.

ACCEPTED! YOU KUNGADO MAY RETURN TO YOUR VILLAGE.

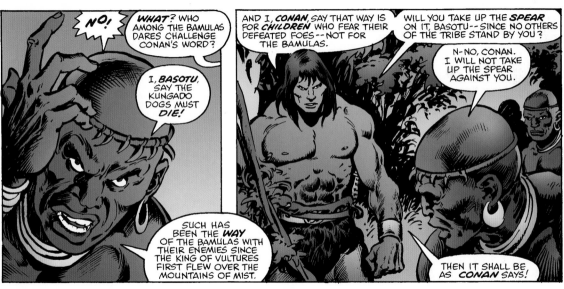

NO!

WHAT? WHO AMONG THE BAMULAS DARES CHALLENGE CONAN'S WORD?

I, *BASOTU*, SAY THE KUNGADO DOGS MUST *DIE!*

SUCH HAS BEEN THE *WAY* OF THE BAMULAS WITH THEIR ENEMIES SINCE THE KING OF VULTURES FIRST FLEW OVER THE MOUNTAINS OF MIST.

AND I, *CONAN*, SAY THAT WAY IS FOR *CHILDREN* WHO FEAR THEIR DEFEATED FOES--NOT FOR THE BAMULAS.

WILL YOU TAKE UP THE *SPEAR* ON IT, BASOTU--SINCE NO OTHERS OF THE TRIBE STAND BY YOU?

N-NO, CONAN. I WILL NOT TAKE UP THE SPEAR AGAINST YOU.

THEN IT SHALL BE AS *CONAN* SAYS!

SOON, THE CHASTENED KUNGADO ARE GONE FROM SIGHT... AND PICKING UP THEIR DEAD AND WOUNDED, THE TRIUMPHANT BAMULAS HEAD BACK TOWARD THEIR OWN VILLAGE...

YET, CONAN KNOWS THE WARRIOR BASOTU WILL NOT *FOR-GET* THEIR DIS-PUTE THIS DAY...

...AND THAT THE *WITCH-MEN* OF THE TRIBE WILL PICK UP THE SONG, WITH IMMUNITY FROM THE NORTHERNER'S SWORD--

WOE TO THE BAMULAS-- FROM THE DAY A *WHITE DOG* SQUATTED ON THE WAR-CHIEF'S CHAIR!

WOE! WOE!

YOU ALREADY *SAID* THAT, WITCH-MAN...

YET, I DEFEATED YORUBO IN A FAIR FIGHT UNDER THE EYES OF *EKKU*, GOD OF FORTUNE.*

AND, SINCE I BECAME WAR-CHIEF, HAS NOT *TRIBUTE* FLOWED TO THE BAMULAS LIKE WATER TO THE SEA?

NO MATTER! THE GODS WAIT-- THE GODS WATCH-- THE GODS *DECIDE.*

*LAST ISSUE. --ROY.

THE ENIGMATIC WITCH-DOCTORS WILL SAY NO MORE.

THUS, CONAN THE CIMMERIAN *BROODS* THIS FULL-MOON NIGHT, SITTING UPON HIS GREAT HIGH-TUSKED CHAIR...

...AND THINKING THERE MUST BE A *BETTER* WAY TO GOLD AND GLORY...

...THAN LORDING IT OVER SPEAR-WIELDING SAVAGES WHO, HOWEVER BRAVE AND FEARSOME, WILL NEVER BE *HIS* PEOPLE.

NOR, IN TURN, CAN HE EVER BE ONE OF *THEM*, NOT EVEN IF HE WERE TO DWELL AMONG THEM A LIFETIME AND MAKE THEM MASTERS FROM KUSH TO THE FABLED "FIRES OF THE SOUTH."

FOOD THERE IS IN PLENTY...AYE, AND *WOMEN*, IF HE WANTED THEM AT PRESENT.

BUT, HE'S NOT YET FORGOTTEN *BÊLIT*, SHE OF THE DARK EYES AND READY SWORD...

MY THANKS, BELIMA.

AND SO, HE WALKS THE SHADOWED PATHWAY BACK TO HIS HUT... *ALONE.*

44

YET, THOUGH HE'S NOT REMEMBERED THE FACT, HIS HUT IS **NOT** EMPTY--

THE BAMULAS DESERVE NO LESS FELIDA... BUT, I'M NOT YOUR "CHIEFTAIN," NOR NEED YOU CALL ME SUCH.

THE VICTORY-FIRES WRITHE **HIGH** TONIGHT, MY CHIEFTAIN.

I KNOW THAT, MAN OF THE NORTH.

YOU WERE **WIFE** TO YORUBO-- AND, THOUGH BAMULA CUSTOM CALLS FOR YOU TO BE NOW THE MATE OF HIS **SLAYER**--MYSELF-- I WOULD CLAIM NO WOMAN AGAINST HER WILL.

STILL, YORUBO IS DEAD, OF HIS OWN MAKING...AND I YET **LIVE**...

...AND A WOMAN NEEDS A **HUSBAND**, EVEN IF IT IS THE SLAYER OF HER FORMER MATE.

YOU ARE A GOOD MAN, MY CHIEFTAIN... AND I SHALL NOT SPURN YOU.

GRIM-EYED, CONAN WATCHES FELIDA...BUT MAKES NO MOVE TOWARD HER.

AND, ERE LONG, SHE SLEEPS.

ONE NIGHT SOON, PERHAPS, HE WILL COME TO HER AMONG THE SKINS...FOR SHE IS FAIR, AND HE HAS BEEN LONG FROM THE COMPANY OF WOMEN.

AYE, PERHAPS... SOON...

...BUT NOT TONIGHT.

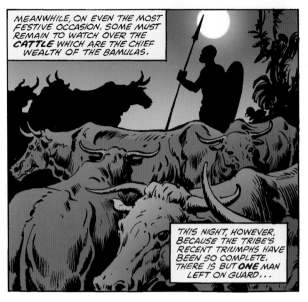

MEANWHILE, ON EVEN THE MOST FESTIVE OCCASION, SOME MUST REMAIN TO WATCH OVER THE **CATTLE** WHICH ARE THE CHIEF WEALTH OF THE BAMULAS.

THIS NIGHT, HOWEVER, BECAUSE THE TRIBE'S RECENT TRIUMPHS HAVE BEEN SO COMPLETE, THERE IS BUT **ONE** MAN LEFT ON GUARD...

45

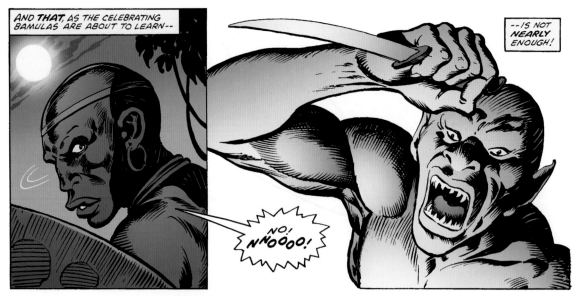

AND *THAT*, AS THE CELEBRATING BAMULAS ARE ABOUT TO LEARN--

--IS NOT *NEARLY* ENOUGH!

NO! NNOOOO!

YET, EVEN AS THE THIRSTING KNIFE DIGS DEEP INTO THE HAPLESS WARRIOR'S CHEST, ENDING HIS TOO-SHORT LIFE--

--AND EVEN AS *MORE* SHADOWY, QUASI-HUMAN FIGURES SHAMBLE FORTH FROM THE JUNGLE NIGHT--

AAAAAA

--A SAYING WHICH WAS OLD WHEN ATLANTIS SANK IS PROVED TRUE ONCE MORE--

"LIFE IS BLOOD... AND BLOOD, LIFE."

THE HERDSMAN'S BRIEF SHRIEK OF TERROR AND PAIN, HOWEVER, HAS NOT GONE UNHEARD IN THE NEARBY VILLAGE...

HO, BAMULAS!

WAKE UP, DAMN YOUR DRUNKEN BONES!

UP, WARRIORS-- I WANT EVERY MAN WHO CAN HEFT A *SPEAR*!!

AYE, WAR-CHIEF...BUT *WHAT*--?

DIDN'T YOU *HEAR*? THAT CRY CAME FROM HIM WHO GUARDS THE *HERD*!

SO VITAL ARE THE CATTLE TO THE BAMULAS, BOTH AS SUBSTANCE AND AS SYMBOL, THAT CONAN'S ADMONITION **SOBERS UP** ALL BUT THE MOST INEBRIATED OF THE SPEARMEN...

AND, MOMENTS LATER, THEY RUSH HEADLONG INTO THE SURROUNDING NIGHT.

BUT, AS THEY REACH THE NEARBY HERD-COMPOUND...

AIEEE! TH-THIS CANNOT BE!

FLEE, BROTHERS OF THE BAMULA TRIBE--

THE CATTLE-STEALERS--THEY ARE THE **MEN WHO DRINK BLOOD!**

FLEE, FOR THEY ARE THE **UNDEAD ONES**-- THE ONES WHO **CANNOT BE SLAIN!**

ON THE INSTANT, THE WARRIORS BEGIN TO **FALL BACK**-- WITHOUT CASTING SO MUCH AS A SINGLE SPEAR--

BUT, **ONE** AMONG THEM THERE IS WHO LEAPS TO THE FORE--

I FEAR THE SUPER-NATURAL AS MUCH AS **ANY**-- AND HAVE ENCOUNTERED IT MORE THAN **MOST.**

I **DON'T** THINK THOSE POINT-EARED DOGS ARE **TRUE VAMPIRES**--

--AND, CROM HELP ME-- **I WAS RIGHT!**

AGGK

SO HARD IS THE CIMMERIAN'S WEAPON HURLED THAT IT **IMPALES** THE GAUNT INTER-LOPER AGAINST THE COW BEHIND HIM--

--HIS HEAD AND BODY SLUMPING **LIFELESS** ACROSS THE STRICKEN ANIMAL!

NOW DO YOU SEE, BROTHERS OF THE SPEAR?

IT IS **NOT** THE UNDEAD YOU FIGHT-- BUT MEN! **MEN!**

MEN WHO CAN **BLEED** AS MUCH BLOOD AS THEY MAY **DRINK!**

NOW *COME!* LET US SHOW THEM HOW THE MEN OF THE BAMULA PROTECT THEIR STOCK!

OUR WAR-CHIEFTAIN SPEAKS TRUE WORDS!

AYE! LET US PAY THE TRESPASSERS BACK FOR LONG MOONS OF *DECEIT* AND *THEFT!*

BEFORE THE RENEWED CHARGE OF THE OUTRAGED *TRIBESMEN,* THE INVADERS FADE BACK INTO THE NIGHT-SHROUDED JUNGLE--

AND SOON, ALL ARE QUITE *VANISHED* FROM SIGHT AND SOUND--

--ALL SAVE *ONE:*

BY EKKU AND AJUJO! NEVER BEFORE HAS ANYONE LIVING SEEN A WARRIOR OF THE *BLOOD MEN* LYING DEAD.

PERHAPS IT IS ONLY THAT OUR WAR-CHIEF'S *MAGIC* IS STRONGER THAN THEIRS...

NO! THEY ARE *MEN,* I TELL YOU-- NO MAGIC TO THEM!

THEIR TEETH ARE *FILED,* AS I'VE HEARD TELL THEY DO IN DISTANT *DARFAR...*

AND, I'LL ADMIT I DON'T UNDERSTAND JUST WHY THEIR *EARS* ARE POINTED, LIKE THOSE OF A JUNGLE BAT, BUT--

AAIIEE

A *CRY*-- FROM WITHIN OUR VERY *VILLAGE!*

A *WOMAN'S* CRY--

FELIDA!

WITHIN INSTANTS, THE SNARLING BAR-BARIAN HAS HURLED HIMSELF PAST THE QUIVERING *GATE-GUARDS*, STILL TOO FEAR-STRICKEN TO ANSWER THE DESPERATE CALL FOR HELP--

--AND INTO HIS OWN *HUT!*

SNEAKED IN THE BACK WAY TO FIGHT WITH *WOMEN*, DID YOU?

WELL, TRY A *MAN*, INSTEAD!

THE INTRUDERS, UNUSED TO SUCH OPPOSITION, ARE A SPLIT-SECOND *SLOW* IN RESPONDING WITH RAISED WEAPONS--

--WHILE A STRIKING *ADDER* COULD SCARCELY REACT MORE SWIFTLY THAN DOES *CONAN THE CIMMERIAN!*

GGNNG

AND, WHEN A *SECOND* OF THE MARAUDING TRIO FALLS BEFORE A FIST THAT SEEMS MADE OF HYRKANIAN STEEL--

UNHN

--THE *THIRD* DARES NOT STAND AGAINST HIM ALONE, BUT SEEKS REFUGE IN HEADLONG *FLIGHT.*

HE DOES NOT FIND IT.

AAAAAA AAAAAAAAaa

SURPRISINGLY, HOWEVER, IT WAS NOT A SPEAR THROWN BY CONAN THAT FELLED THE INTERLOPER...

BASOTU DID IT! BASOTU SLEW THE BLOOD-DRINKER!

SAVE ONLY FOR OUR WAR-CHIEF, BASOTU IS SURELY THE MIGHTIEST BAMULA OF ALL!

CONAN SENSES TROUBLE FOR HIMSELF IN HIS POTENTIAL RIVAL'S BRAVERY... BUT, EVEN AN AMBITIOUS BARBARIAN CANNOT CONCERN HIMSELF WITH EVERYTHING AT ONCE, AND SO...

WELL, BAMULAS? YOU HAVE SEEN HOW ONE OF YOU, AS WELL AS I, CAN KILL THESE DOGS.

BEHOLD THIS PITIFUL WRETCH I LET LIVE-- SO YOU CAN SEE HOW BASELESS HAVE BEEN YOUR FEARS!

HE SPEAKS TRULY, MEN OF THE BAMULAS...

IT IS ONE OF THE WISE OLD MEN OF THE TRIBE WHO NOW STEPS FORWARD...

I HAVE LONG KNOWN THE TRUTH OF "THE MEN WHO DRINK BLOOD"-- BUT NO ONE WOULD HEED MY WORDS.

THEY WILL NOW, OLD MAN, SPEAK.

THEY DWELL IN A LAND SUNWARD OF OUR OWN...

"...AND, SINCE MY GRANDFATHER'S DAY, THEY HAVE BEEN AS THEY ARE...

"...DRINKING MOSTLY THE LIFEBLOOD OF CATTLE THEY EITHER BRED OR STOLE."

THEY ARE NOT TRUE *DRELLIKS,** OF COURSE... EVEN THOUGH THEY FILE THEIR TEETH TO POINTS, AND SHAPE THE EARS OF THEIR CHILDREN TO RESEMBLE THOSE OF THE BLOOD-DRINKING *BATS.*

THEY *DO*, DO THEY?

*BAMULA WORD FOR VAMPIRE. --ROY.

"*AYE.* TRUE *DRELLIKS,* OF COURSE, CAN BE SLAIN--THE STORIES SAY-- ONLY BY *BEHEADING* THEM AND DRIVING *WOOD* OR *METAL* THROUGH THEIR EVIL, INHUMAN HEARTS.

"IN DAYS PAST, ON THE RARE TIMES WHEN ONE OF THE '*MEN WHO DRINK BLOOD*' WAS SLAIN, HE WAS BE-HEADED AT ONCE-- AND SO THE LEGEND PERSISTED, WITH NOTHING TO CONTRADICT IT."

MY FATHER, YOU SEE, WAS ONCE A *SLAVE* IN THEIR COMPOUND, WHICH SURROUNDS A HILL WHICH IS A MAZE OF CAVES... AND HE TOLD ME THIS.

DID HE ALSO TELL YOU *WHY* THEY PRE- TEND TO BE *DRELLIKS?*

NAY, BUT IT MUST BE MERELY TO AFFRIGHT THEIR *FOES*, MUST IT NOT?

I SUPPOSE SO. THANKS, OLD ONE.

ARE YOU ALL RIGHT, FELIDA?

YES, MY CHIEFTAIN... THANKS TO YOU.

GOOD. WHEN I RETURN, WE WILL TALK *MORE* ABOUT... THAT WHICH YOU SPOKE OF, BEFORE.

THAT WOULD MAKE MY HEART SING, MY CHIEFTAIN.

WE GO, THEN, CONAN, TO FIND THE *VILLAGE* OF THE "*MEN WHO DRINK BLOOD*"?

AYE! WE'LL TEACH THEM THEY'D BEST GO BACK TO DRINKING THE BLOOD OF *CATTLE*, NOT--

O *MIGHTIEST OF ALL THE BAMULA*-- LET ME GO *WITH* YOU, I PRAY YOU!

I COULDN'T *TRUST* A DOG LIKE YOU-- AND BE- SIDES, WE WOULD TRAVEL MOSTLY BY THE *DAYLIGHT* YOU BLOOD- SUCKERS SHUN.

WHAT? *YOU*-- WHO ARE *ONE* OF THEM?!

OH, BUT THAT IS ONLY BECAUSE WE ARE KEPT *FROM* THE LIGHT, FROM BIRTH ON.

OUR *EYES* ARE AS DELICATE AS OUR WHISPER-LIKE *VOICES.*

WE HAVE THESE *SMOKY CRYSTALS*-- YOU SEE?-- FOR THOSE TIMES WHEN WE MUST WALK IN THE SUN.

I AM *ASHIDO.* YOU WILL TAKE ME WITH YOU, *YES?*

I WILL TAKE YOU WITH US, *YES*-- BUT ONLY SO THAT YOU CAN SHOW US THE *SAFEST APPROACH* TO THE CAVE-VILLAGE OF THE *DRELLIKS*.

SERVE ME WELL, AND I'LL LET YOU LIVE-- CROSS US, AND I WILL PUT A *SPEAR* THROUGH YOUR SHIVERING SPINE!

OH, ASHIDO KNOWS THAT *WELL*, MIGHTY ONE! I WILL BE *FAITHFUL.*

WITH THESE WORDS, CONAN LEADS HIS BRAVEST FIGHTERS INTO THE JUNGLE-- TOWARD THE LAND OF THE MEN WHO DRINK BLOOD.

THE BAMULA, FOR THEIR PART, ARE UNEASY, FEARFUL-- BUT THEY WILL NOT LET *CONAN* AND *BASUTO* SEEM MORE COURAGEOUS THAN THEY.

BESIDES, VALIANT THOUGH THEY BE IN BATTLE, THEY DO NOT DARE TO FACE THE CIMMERIAN'S *SCORN.*

LONG DAYS ARE SPENT IN THE TREK THROUGH RAIN FOREST AND DENSE UNDERBRUSH, UNTIL, ONE DAY WHEN THE SUN IS HIGH--

THERE, O GREATEST OF BAMULA! YOU SEE? ASHIDO HAS DONE AS HE PROMISED.

YONDER, MY PEOPLE LIE *SLEEPING* TILL NIGHTFALL, WHEN THEY WILL HAVE *STRENGTH* TO VENTURE OUTSIDE.

AYE, I'VE SEEN HOW DREAMY AND *SLOW* YOU SEEM DURING DAY-LIGHT.

IT IS THE *WAY* OF THE *DRELLIKS*, MIGHTY ONE.

NOW *HURRY!* YOU CAN SLIT ALL THEIR THROATS AND MY BROTHERS WILL WAKEN IN THE LAND OF THE *TRUE DEAD.*

WHERE *YOU* WILL BE WAITING, JACKAL, TO *WELCOME* THEM!

BASUTO-- *STOP!!*

P-PLEASE, MIGHTY ONE-- I HAVE BEEN *FAITHFUL--!*

I SWORE TO LET THE DOG *LIVE*, IF HE DID NOT SEEK TO BETRAY US-- AND I *KEEP* MY WORD, EVEN TO DRELLIKS.

THEN YOU ARE A *FOOL*, WAR-CHIEF...AT LEAST IN THIS WAY!

THAT MAY BE... BUT, FOR THE PRESENT, HE *LIVES.*

SILENCE REIGNS SUPREME NOW, AS CONAN ALONE DRAWS NEAR THE GREAT WALL OF STAKES, CRUDE GRAPPLING-HOOK IN HAND...

...TO SCALE IT, WITH SUCH EASE AS ONLY A HILL-BORN CIMMERIAN MAY KNOW.

STILL, HE ALMOST WISHES THERE WERE AN UNSUSPECTING GUARD OR TWO AT THE TOP TO SLAY.

AS IT IS, THIS HAS ALL THE EARMARKS OF AN AMBUSH.

STILL, NO ONE APPEARS... SO THE HUGE COMPOUND GATE IS SOON SWUNG OPEN...

ENTER-- BUT KEEP STILL!

LET NO BAMULA'S VOICE BE LOUDER THAN ASHIDO'S HOARSE WHISPER!

YOU SEE, MIGHTY PROTECTOR? THE DRELLIKS ALL SLEEP YONDER, IN THE GREAT CAVE-- WHERE OUR KING DWELLS.

KING, EH? WELL, PERHAPS THE DRELLIKS WILL HAVE A NEW SOVEREIGN, COME NIGHT.

PERHAPS, COME, NOW...

YOU SHOULD HAVE NO TROUBLE SLAYING MY BROTHERS, ERE THEY ARE ROUSED.

BROTHERS? WHAT OF YOUR WOMEN? YOU NEVER--

WOMEN? WHAT USE HAVE WE OF WOMEN, SAVE WHEN BREEDING-TIME COMES UPON US?

WE SLAY THEM LATER, AS WE DO ALL GIRL-CHILDREN.

WE ARE A WARRIOR RACE.

¿HUHN!? YOU ALMOST MAKE ME SORRY I STAYED BASUTO'S HAND.

NO SUNLIGHT WINDS ITS WAY INTO THE SHADOW-HAUNTED CAVERN...

NOR IS ANY SOUND HEARD, SAVE ONLY THE REGULAR BREATHING OF THE SLEEPING *DRELLIKS* HERE SPRAWLED IN STRANGE PROFUSION UPON SLAB AND BOULDER.

CONAN AND BASUTO ARE FIRST TO FOLLOW THEIR CRINGING CAPTIVE INSIDE, WEAPONS AT THE READY.

BEHIND THEM, THE OTHER BAMULA TENSE-- AS ASHIDO POINTS A SKELETAL FINGER TOWARD *THE NETHER END* OF THE VAST YAWNING CAVE...

...WHERE A TALL GAUNT FIGURE, VEILED IN DARKNESS, SITS UPON A HIDEOUS CARVEN *THRONE.*

BECKONING THE OTHERS TO IMMOBILITY, CONAN TAKES A SINGLE TENTATIVE STEP TOWARD IT.

THEN, WEIRD AND PIERCING *EYES* OPEN, THOUGH THERE IS NO OTHER MOVEMENT FROM THE TOWERING FIGURE--

--AND, JUST AS SWIFTLY, A *HIDDEN GATEWAY* DESCENDS BEHIND THE STARTLED INTRUDERS!

WAR-CHIEF! W-WE ARE TRAPPED HERE!!

HUSH! CONAN SAID TO *WHISPER!* BESIDES, WE STILL HAVE OUR SPEARS.

YET, EVEN AS BASUTO GROWLS THE WORDS, THE NEED FOR SILENCE IS *PAST*...

...AS ALL AROUND THEM, *LITHE DARK SHAPES* RISE SLOWLY, MENACINGLY, LIKE OMINOUS CAVE-FLOWERS UNFOLDING THEIR VENOMOUS PETALS.

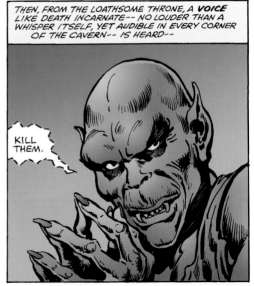

THEN, FROM THE LOATHSOME THRONE, A *VOICE* LIKE DEATH INCARNATE-- NO LOUDER THAN A WHISPER ITSELF, YET AUDIBLE IN EVERY CORNER OF THE CAVERN-- IS HEARD--

KILL THEM.

FROM BEHIND A JUTTING STALAGMITE, A BLEAK FORM LEAPS OUT, AND--

RRGGG

IT *WAS* A TRAP, THEN!

LYING DOG! YOU SWORE THE DRELLIKS SLEPT IN DAYTIME!

THERE IS *NO* DAYTIME HERE, MIGHTIEST OF FOOLS-- ONLY *NIGHT*--

--NIGHT SUCH AS I WILL SEND YOU *SHRIEKING* TO!!

UHH--?

THE DRELLIK'S HAND IS *QUICK*, REACHING FOR THE DAGGER OF A BAMULA WHO, CONFUSED BY EVENTS, HAS STEPPED TOO NEAR HIM...

BUT *CONAN'S* REFLEXES ARE AS UNERRING AS EVER!

AAAA

TO MY *TRUE* MASTER-- I HAVE BEEN *FAITH-FUL*--

--EVEN UNTO THE *TRUE DEATH*--!

THEN, EVEN AS ASHIDO'S LIFELESS CORPSE FALLS, THE GAUNT GIANT ON THE DAIS *RISES*...

YOU WILL MAKE GOOD *CATTLE* FOR US, MEN OF THE BAMULA.

CONAN AND HIS WARRIORS ARE FODDER FOR *NO* MAN, DOG--

--LEAST OF ALL, FOR ONE WHO STYLES HIMSELF ONE OF THE *UNDEAD*, MERELY TO STEAL THEIR *CATTLE!*

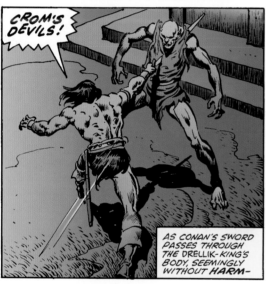

CROM'S *DEVILS!*

AS CONAN'S SWORD PASSES THROUGH THE DRELLIK-KING'S BODY, SEEMINGLY WITHOUT *HARM*--

--HE SUDDENLY REALIZES THE TRUTH--

THIS IS NO STRUTTING MASQUER HE FACES-- BUT A *REAL VAMPIRE!*

THE THOUGHT FILLS HIM WITH SUDDEN *PANIC*, AS REAL AS EVEN THAT OF HIS FIGHTERS--

YET, ALMOST AS QUICKLY, HE *LASHES OUT*--

--BEATING HAMMERLIKE, YET STRANGELY *INEFFECTUAL* FISTS AGAINST THE ELDRITCH BEING BEFORE HIM.

U NG N

THEN, A SINGLE TALONED *HAND* CLOSES ON THE BARBARIAN'S TENSED THROAT--

--AND CONAN KNOWS, PERHAPS FOR THE FIRST TIME, THE FEELING WHICH *HIS* MIGHTY-THEWED STRENGTH HAS INDUCED IN LESSER MORTALS--

THE SENSATION OF TOTAL, UN-RELIEVED *HELP-LESSNESS!*

ARRR

THEN, AS THE BRONZED OUTLANDER LIES UNMOVING...

SURRENDER, INTERLOPERS... OR I SHALL TEAR YOU, ONE BY ONE, LIMB FROM LIMB!

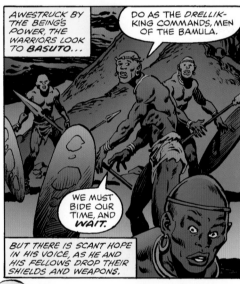

AWESTRUCK BY THE BEING'S POWER, THE WARRIORS LOOK TO *BASUTO...*

DO AS THE DRELLIK-KING COMMANDS, MEN OF THE BAMULA.

WE MUST BIDE OUR TIME, AND *WAIT.*

BUT THERE IS SCANT HOPE IN HIS VOICE, AS HE AND HIS FELLOWS DROP THEIR SHIELDS AND WEAPONS.

NEXT MOMENT, AS EFFORTLESSLY AS A CHILD MIGHT LIFT A BROKEN BUT VALUED DOLL, THE GAUNT DRELLIK-KING LIFTS CONAN'S MASSIVE FRAME FROM THE COLD, CLAMMY STONES...

...AND CARRIES HIM BACK INTO THE DEEPER, EVEN DARKER RECESSES OF THE CAVERN, WHERE IT IS EVER *NIGHT...*

...BOTH FOR THE *EYE,* AND FOR THE *SOUL....!*

NEXT ISSUE: IMMORTALITY-- OR *DEATH!*

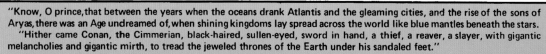

"Know, O prince, that between the years when the oceans drank Atlantis and the gleaming cities, and the rise of the sons of Aryas, there was an Age undreamed of, when shining kingdoms lay spread across the world like blue mantles beneath the stars.
"Hither came Conan, the Cimmerian, black-haired, sullen-eyed, sword in hand, a thief, a reaver, a slayer, with gigantic melancholies and gigantic mirth, to tread the jeweled thrones of the Earth under his sandaled feet."
—The Nemedian Chronicles.

Stan Lee PRESENTS: CONAN THE BARBARIAN®

BRIDE OF THE VAMPIRE!

MIGHTY OF THEW, STRONG OF SINEW IS *CONAN* THE CIMMERIAN, NOW WAR-CHIEF OF THE SAVAGE BAMULA TRIBE, EAST OF THE BLACK COAST...

YET, EVEN HIS IRON STRENGTH HAS PROVEN BUT A STRAW IN THE JUNGLE WINDS AGAINST THE *KING OF THE DRELLIKS--* A LOOMING, GAUNT VAMPIRE WHO OVERCAME THE BRONZED BARBARIAN AS IF HE WERE BUT A WAYWARD CHILD.

WAIT YOU *HERE,* MY *DRELLIKS--* FOR YOUR MASTER HAS BUSINESS WITH THIS WHITE-SKINNED WARRIOR...

ROY THOMAS
WRITER/ EDITOR

JOHN BUSCEMA & ERNIE CHAN
ILLUSTRATORS

JOE ROSEN
LETTERER

JIM SHOOTER
CONSULTING EDITOR

FEATURING THE HERO CREATED BY
ROBERT E. HOWARD

HIS **MEN**, HOWEVER, BELONG TO **YOU.**

YOU KNOW WHAT TO DO WITH THEM...!

AND INDEED THEY **DO.**

THUS, WHEN THEIR IMMORTAL KING HAS DISAPPEARED INTO HIS OWN PRIVATE CAVERN...

...THEY TURN THEIR ATTENTION TO THE DEFEATED **BAMULA.**

THEY ARE NOT **TRUE** VAMPIRES, THESE DRELLIKS...THESE *"MEN WHO DRINK BLOOD"...*

STILL, THEY HAVE **WEAPONS,** WHICH CONAN'S SURRENDERED WARRIORS DO NOT.

BASUTO-- SHALL WE MAKE A **STAND** AGAINST THE DRELLIKS?

NO, TUMARA, IT WOULD BE A **SLAUGHTER.**

AND WHAT **ELSE** WILL THEY DO TO US-- BUT SLAY US, AND DRINK **OUR** BLOOD, AS THEY HAVE EVER DRUNK THAT OF CATTLE?

IN THERE, DOGS...TILL WE HAVE **NEED** OF YOU.

AND NOT A MAN OF THE BAMULA BUT KNOWS **WHAT** THAT NEED SHALL BE.

THEN DOES **BASUTO,** WHO ALONE OF HIS FIERCE TRIBESMEN IS CONAN'S RIVAL, KNOW THE ULTIMATE HOPELESSNESS OF THE FALLEN WARRIOR--

HIS LIFE, PERHAPS HIS VERY **SOUL**.... AND THAT OF HIS FELLOW BAMULA...

...DEPENDENT UPON ONE WHO LIES SENSELESS IN A NEARBY CAVE.

YOU ARE **STRONG,** MAN OF THE PALE NORTH...

...STRONG FAR BEYOND **ANY** MORTAL I HAVE EVER MET, BE HE DARK OR LIGHT.

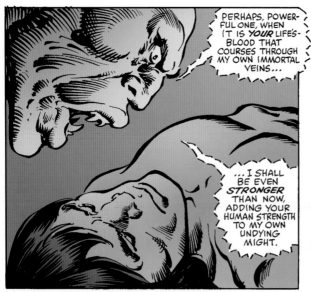

PERHAPS, POWERFUL ONE, WHEN IT IS *YOUR* LIFE'S-BLOOD THAT COURSES THROUGH MY OWN IMMORTAL VEINS...

...I SHALL BE EVEN *STRONGER* THAN NOW, ADDING YOUR HUMAN STRENGTH TO MY OWN UNDYING MIGHT.

LIKE HELL YOU WILL!

ARRR

YOU... WAKEN *QUICKLY*, OUTLANDER.

IT'S BEEN MY WAY.

BESIDES, YOUR *BREATH* WOULD ROUSE EVEN A *GRAVESPAWN* LIKE YOURSELF.

NOW, DO WE *FIGHT* MORE, OR--?

WHAT DO *YOU* KNOW, NORTH-BORN ONE, OF THE GRAVE-- OR OF THOSE WHO HAVE LONG *DEFIED* THEIR OWN?

EVEN *I*, WITHOUT EFFORT, CAN SCARCELY RE-CALL THAT TIME WHEN I STOOD ON THE *OTHER* SIDE OF YAWNING DEATH...

"...AND WHEN I WAS *K'CHAMA*, GREATEST WARRIOR OF A TRIBE FAR TO THE EAST.

"I WANDERED THE JUNGLE BY *NIGHT* THEN, IN SEARCH OF GLORY...

"...FINDING DARK-WINGED *DEATH* INSTEAD!

SKREEE

"DEATH, IN THE FORM OF A GIANT, BLOOD-SUCKING *BAT* WHICH SWOOPED DOWN UPON ME FROM OUT OF A SWOLLEN MOON!

"MY SPEARPOINT DID NOT STOP IT...

"AND IT WAS ONLY WHEN THE WEAPON'S *SHAFT* WAS THRUST THROUGH THE BEAST'S HEART, AS WELL, THAT *LIFE* FLED FROM IT...

"...IF LIFE IT CAN BE CALLED.

"THEN, AS I WITH-DREW MY SPEAR, MY OWN HEART GREW *FAINT* WITHIN ME.

"FOR, THE SLAIN BAT SUDDENLY BECAME... A SLAIN *MAN.*

"HE HAD BEEN A *VAMPIRE*... A *DRELLIK.*

"AND, BECAUSE HIS *FANGS* AND *TALONS* HAD RAKED ME MANY TIMES ERE HE PERISHED, *I* SOON DIED A DEATH, TOO... OF A SORT...

"...RISING AGAIN, THREE NIGHTS LATER, AS A *TRUE* DRELLIK.

"AND I THIRSTED.

"THAT THIRST WAS SLAKED BY THE BLOOD OF A STRAY *BULL*, FIRST, AND I ADDED ITS STRENGTH TO MY OWN.

"BUT, I SOON SOUGHT OUT EVEN *FIERCER* PREY.

GNARR

"MY SINEWS, NOW, WERE GREATER THAN *ANY* MORTAL'S.

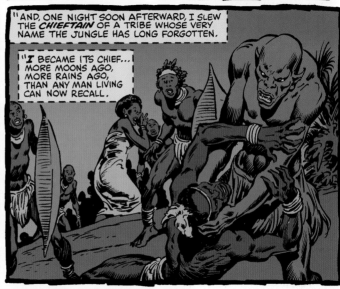

"AND, ONE NIGHT SOON AFTERWARD, I SLEW THE *CHIEFTAIN* OF A TRIBE WHOSE VERY NAME THE JUNGLE HAS LONG FORGOTTEN.

"*I* BECAME ITS CHIEF... MORE MOONS AGO, MORE RAINS AGO, THAN ANY MAN LIVING CAN NOW RECALL.

"I HAD NO USE FOR *WOMEN*, SAVE AS THEY WOULD BREED NEW WARRIORS FOR MY ADOPTED TRIBE, WHICH I NOW CALLED THE *DRELLIKS.*

"THE *MEN* CAME UNDER MY HYPNO-TIC INFLUENCE, WITH NO REAL *WILL* SAVE MY OWN.

"I COMMANDED THEIR *TEETH* BE FILED FROM THEIR DAY OF MANHOOD...

"...THEIR *EARS* POINTED BY CEREMONIES TAKING PLACE IN CHILDHOOD.

"I TAUGHT THEM TO DRINK THAT FOR WHICH *I* THIRSTED..."

...AND THUS WAS BORN THE LEGEND OF THE *MEN WHO DRINK BLOOD.*

YOU *RE-MADE* THEM, THEN... IN YOUR OWN IMAGE?

AYE, SO FAR AS I *COULD*...

"STILL, THEY WERE *MEN*, NOT TRUE VAMPIRES...EVEN THEIR *SENSITIVITY TO LIGHT* ONLY SOMETHING I INSTILLED IN THEIR SONS BY FORBIDDING THEM TO GO FORTH INTO DAYLIGHT.

"THUS, AS THEY DIED, ONE BY ONE, I FELT MORE ALONE...MORE *LONELY* THAN BEFORE,"

THEN WHY DIDN'T YOU CHANGE SOME OF THEM *INTO* TRUE VAMPIRES-- AS THAT BAT-THING DID TO *YOU*?

BECAUSE THEY WERE... *NOT WORTHY.*

BECAUSE I HAVE MET *NO* MAN, OF ANY COLOR, I WOULD SHARE THE *SECRET OF ETERNITY* WITH...

...TILL *YOU.*

ME!? YOU MUST BE *MAD,* DRELLIK!

I'LL DIE A *WARRIOR,* WHEN DIE I MUST-- BUT I'LL NOT BECOME AN *UNDEAD CONSORT* TO A *MONSTER!*

I HAVE *HEARD* OF YOU, CONAN, WAR-CHIEF OF THE BAMULA...

...AND I CAN GUESS YOU MEAN TO BUILD A *BLACK EMPIRE,* WITH THAT FIERCE TRIBE AS ITS HUB.

BUT, THEY ARE AS UNWORTHY OF *YOU* AS MY FOLLOWERS OF *ME.*

THINK OF WHAT WE COULD ACCOMPLISH *TOGETHER,* YOU AND I--

"--TWIN *DRELLIKS,* LORDING IT OVER THE *MEN WHO DRINK BLOOD*-- YET POSSESSED OF *REAL* SUPERNATURAL POWER, NOT MERELY ITS APPEARANCE.

"YOU ARE *STRONG,* WHITE MAN! IMAGINE HOW MUCH STRONGER YOU SHALL BE, HOW MUCH MORE FEARSOME, WHEN YOU HAVE DIED AND RETURNED AS A *TRUE DRELLIK!*

"YOU SHALL BE AS *STRONG* AS YOU WILL BE *IMMORTAL!*"

WE SHALL STRIDE DOWN THE *AGES*, YOU AND I, WITH--

WHAT--??

BLOOD-SUCKING DOG!

I AM A *MAN*, NOT AN UNDEAD *THING* LIKE YOU! I'LL NEVER--

YOU ARE... VERY *FOOLISH*, OUT-LANDER.

URRK

POWERFUL FINGERS CUT OFF THE CIMMERIAN'S OXYGEN... WITH SKILL ENOUGH THAT HE MERELY *BLACKS OUT*, STILL ALIVE.

I SHOULD HAVE KNOWN THAT ONE WHO'S NOT LIVED LONG ENOUGH TO GROW TRULY WISE WOULD *SPURN* MY OFFER... AT FIRST.

TIME, HOWEVER, IS OF SCANT IMPORTANCE TO ME...

THUS, I SHALL LEAVE YOU *HERE* FOR A WHILE...

...TO *RECONSIDER* YOUR CHOICE OF DEATHS--

AT *MY* HANDS, WITH IMMORTALITY YOUR REWARD...

...OR A *MORTAL* DEATH, THROWN TO MY MEN.

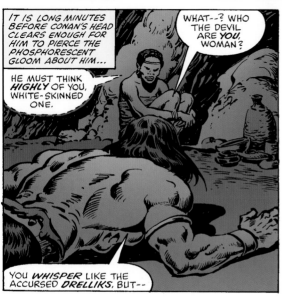

IT IS LONG MINUTES BEFORE CONAN'S HEAD CLEARS ENOUGH FOR HIM TO PIERCE THE PHOSPHORESCENT GLOOM ABOUT HIM...

HE MUST THINK *HIGHLY* OF YOU, WHITE-SKINNED ONE.

WHAT--? WHO THE DEVIL ARE *YOU*, WOMAN?

YOU *WHISPER* LIKE THE ACCURSED *DRELLIKS*, BUT--

-- BUT THEY HAVE *NO WOMEN*, OTHER THAN FOR PURPOSES OF MATING?

THAT IS TRUE-- SAVE WHERE *EESEE* IS CONCERNED.

OBSERVE-- I ALONE, OF ALL WOMEN, HAVE THE *POINTED EARS*, THE *FILED TEETH* OF THE DRELLIKS...

...THOUGH I ALSO HAVE K'CHAMA'S *FANG-MARKS* IN MY NECK, WHICH CAUSE MY WHISPER.

AS I SAID, I AM *EESEE*... *BRIDE* OF K'CHAMA!

BRIDE!? ARE YOU THEN *IMMORTAL*, AS HE CLAIMS TO BE?

N-NO! HE WOULD NOT GRANT ME THAT BOON-- THOUGH HE KNOWS I HAVE *LOVED* HIM FOR MANY YEARS.

LOVE...?

HIS FANGS HAVE KEPT ME *YOUNG* MORE YEARS THAN YOU COULD GUESS.

BUT NOW, AT LAST, I BEGIN TO *AGE*... AND HE TIRES OF ME.

WELL, DON'T WORRY, EESEE! *I'VE* NO INTENTION OF TAKING YOUR PLACE-- IN *ANY* WAY.

BUT-- THIS *ROCK* HE MUST HAVE SHOVED INTO PLACE--!

IF I CAN *ONLY*--!

UNNNHN! NO-- USE!!

OVER THE YEARS-- THE VAMPIRE MUST HAVE *FITTED* THE STONE-- VERY CAREFULLY.

AIR MUST FILTER INTO THIS CAVE... FROM OTHER SOURCES.

HE COULD MOVE THIS STONE-- AYE, AND *EASILY*--

--BUT NOT *I*!

NOT I, DAMN HIM TO A *THOUSAND UNDEAD HELLS!*

THE WORDS ECHO IN THE SMALL CAVERN, RETURNING IN AN INSTANT TO MOCK HIM.

THEN, WHEN IT IS *NIGHT* IN THE OUTER WORLD ONCE MORE...

...SEVERAL OF THE STRONGER FALSE- DRELLIKS ROLL AWAY THE STONE DOOR, AND *CHAIN* THE BARBARIAN...

...AND TAKE HIM BEFORE K'CHAMA.

YES, FIX THE CHAIN FIRMLY TO THE *RING* OF MY THRONE- SLAB!

I'LL MAKE A *PET* OF THE FOOL-- TILL I CAN MAKE OF HIM SOME- THING *MORE*.

THAT'LL BE *NEVER*.

PERHAPS...

...BUT MEANWHILE, WE SHALL AT LEAST HAVE SOMETHING TO *WATCH*...!

N-NO! HELP ME, CONAN--

IN THE NAME OF THE GODS-- *HELP ME!!*

BUT, CONAN CAN HELP NO ONE NOW, NOT EVEN HIMSELF.

HE CAN ONLY *OBSERVE* AS THE MAN WHO FOLLOWED HIM INTO DRELLIK *COUNTRY* IS SLAIN...

...AND THE "MEN WHO DRINK BLOOD"...

...LIVE UP TO THEIR SHADOW-ECHOING *NAME!*

FIRST, THE SLAYER HIMSELF-- AND THEN HIS SHARP-FANGED FELLOWS-- TEAR AT THE DEAD MAN.

IT IS A GRIM SIGHT...

...ONE TO UNNERVE EVEN *CONAN OF CIMMERIA.*

YOU HAVE *ME*, BLOODSUCKER.

LET MY WARRIORS *GO*-- AND THEY'LL NOT TROUBLE YOU AGAIN.

NOT TILL YOU PAY THE *PRICE.*

PAY THE--?!

YET, EVEN AS THE WORDS HURL THEMSELVES FROM HIS LIPS, THE BARBARIAN KNOWS WHAT THE VAMPIRE HAS MEANT.

ALL RIGHT, DOG! I SHALL *WILLINGLY* JOIN YOU... IN YOUR HIDEOUS STATE OF *LIFE IN DEATH.*

BUT FIRST-- THE BAMULA MUST BE *FREED.*

OF COURSE. THEY MEAN NOTHING TO ME.

DRELLIKS! YOU HAVE FEASTED WELL TONIGHT.

NOW, FREE THE OTHERS-- AND LET THEM DEPART!

THERE IS GRUMBLING AMONG THE LESS SATED OF THE HUMAN VAMPIRES...

BUT, THEY HAVE KNOWN THE WRATH OF THEIR IMMORTAL KING BEFORE... AND WISH NOT TO KNOW IT AGAIN.

THUS, WITHIN MINUTES, THE STARTLED BAMULA FIND THE DOORWAY OF THEIR FILTHY CELL OPEN TO THEM...

AND, PICKING UP THEIR WEAPONS WHERE THEY DROPPED THEM, THEY RUSH OFF INTO THE NIGHT.

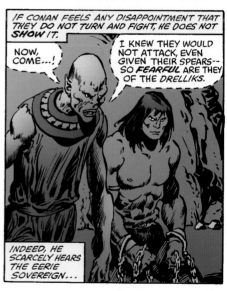

IF CONAN FEELS ANY DISAPPOINTMENT THAT THEY DO NOT TURN AND FIGHT, HE DOES NOT SHOW IT.

NOW, COME...!

I KNEW THEY WOULD NOT ATTACK, EVEN GIVEN THEIR SPEARS-- SO FEARFUL ARE THEY OF THE DRELLIKS.

INDEED, HE SCARCELY HEARS THE EERIE SOVEREIGN...

FOR, HE IS THINKING OF THE GOOD TIMES... AND THE LOVE... HE HAS KNOWN IN HIS DAY.

A MAN CAN ASK ONLY SO MUCH OUT OF LIFE, CONAN MUSES.

STILL, HE COULD WISH HE'D HAD TIME TO DRINK HIS FILL FROM THE CUP OF THE LIVING.

THERE! I HAVE ROLLED THE STONE AWAY FROM THE CAVERN WE TWO SHALL SHARE.

AND WHAT OF THE WOMAN INSIDE?

SHE HAS SERVED YOU WELL OVER THE YEARS, I'LL WARRANT.

AYE, I SUPPOSE SHE HAS...

WHAT *OF* IT? I'VE NO MORE USE FOR HER; I'LL LET YOU MAKE *YOUR* FIRST *DRELLIK*-MEAL OF HER LATER, IF YOU WISH.

ELSE, I'LL MAKE ONE LAST, FULL FEAST OF HER *MYSELF*, IF YOU--

NO, BY CROM! YOU'LL LET HER *GO*, OR OUR BARGAIN IS *OFF*!

AGREED. WHAT CARE *I*?

THEN WHAT DO YOU CARE THAT I JOIN YOU *WILLINGLY* AS A TRUE *DRELLIK*-- WHEN YOU COULD SIMPLY SLAY ME WHEN-EVER YOU *WISHED*?

AYE, THAT I COULD-- BUT MY HOLD ON YOU WOULD NOT BE *BINDING* AFTER YOU, TOO, BECAME A *DRELLIK*.

BUT YOU ARE A *WARRIOR BORN*-- AND I SENSE THAT A *VOW* YOU MAKE, NOT TO HARM ME WHEN YOU ARE AS POWERFUL AS I, WILL BE AS BINDING ON YOU IN *DEATH* AS IN LIFE.

YOU... READ ME *WELL*, YOU BLOATED LEECH.

AS *YOU* SHALL BE, ERE LONG.

WELL? *MAKE* THE VOW, THEN-- AND I'LL TURN THE WOMAN LOOSE IN THE *JUNGLE*, TO MAKE HER WAY BACK TO HER PEOPLE!

THEY SHALL BE THE LAST *HUMAN* WORDS YOU SHALL EVER--- *UNNH!*

EH? WHAT THE *DEVIL*--?

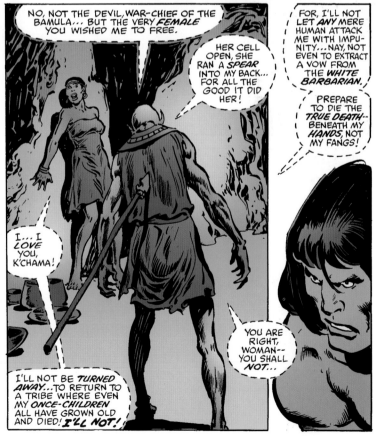

NO, NOT THE DEVIL, WAR-CHIEF OF THE BAMULA... BUT THE VERY *FEMALE* YOU WISHED ME TO FREE.

HER CELL OPEN, SHE RAN A *SPEAR* INTO MY BACK... FOR ALL THE GOOD IT DID HER!

I... I *LOVE* YOU, K'CHAMA!

I'LL NOT BE *TURNED AWAY*...TO RETURN TO A TRIBE WHERE EVEN MY *ONCE-CHILDREN* ALL HAVE GROWN OLD AND DIED! *I'LL NOT!*

FOR, I'LL NOT LET *ANY* MERE HUMAN ATTACK ME WITH IMPU-NITY...NAY, NOT EVEN TO EXTRACT A VOW FROM THE *WHITE BARBARIAN*.

PREPARE TO DIE THE *TRUE DEATH*-- BENEATH MY *HANDS*, NOT MY FANGS!

YOU ARE RIGHT, WOMAN-- YOU SHALL *NOT*...

DO WHAT YOU *WILL* WITH HER, YOU BLOOD-DRINKING SCUM--

--BUT *I'LL* NOT BE HERE TO WATCH IT!

YOU *DARE* NOT! YOU SWORE TO WILLINGLY *JOIN* ME...!

MAYBE SO, BUT I DIDN'T SAY *WHEN*.

COME LOOK ME UP WHEN I'M *EIGHTY* OR SO!

AAIIEE

SO-- I *MISJUDGED* YOU, IT SEEMS.

YOU ARE *NOT* WORTHY OF ME, AFTER ALL.

AWAY, FEMALE! YOU CONCERN ME NO MORE THAN THE *SPEAR* THAT JUTS FROM MY BACK.

IT IS THE *WHITE BARBARIAN* I WANT-- AND WHITE STILL HE *SHALL* BE, WHEN I HAVE DRUNK HIS LAST *LIFE'S-BLOOD!*

MEANWHILE, CONAN IS ALREADY AMONG THE MAN-DRELLIKS--

ARRRH

OUT OF MY *WAY*, YOU DAMNED VERMIN!

--USING HIS CHAIN LIKE A *FLAIL* AGAINST THEM.

NO WAY I CAN SCALE THE *WOODEN* WALLS BEFORE THEY'D GET ME, BUT-- THOSE *VINES!*

THEY LEAD STRAIGHT UP THE *CLIFF!*

BETTER TO MEET MY END BATTLING ON SOME ROCKY *LEDGE* AGAINST THAT UNDEAD HORDE--

--THAN WAITING AROUND LIKE A *SHEEP* RIPE FOR SLAUGHTER!

THEN, AS HE BEHOLDS BOTH THE IMMORTAL K'CHAMA AND HIS DE-FORMED FOLLOWERS RUSHING OUT OF THE GREAT CAVE AFTER HIM, CONAN SNARLS AT THE TAUNTING *MEMORY* OF WHAT HE HAS DONE--

BLOOD-OATHS ARE MEANT TO BE *KEPT*-- AND CONAN MEANT TO KEEP *HIS*, FOR ALL THAT IT REVOLTED AND REVULSED HIM.

HE CURSES HIM-SELF INWARDLY TO REALIZE THAT HE STILL *WOULD* KEEP IT-- AND NOT ONLY WHEN HE HAS ONE FOOT IN AN OLD MAN'S *GRAVE*, EITHER.

BUT, HE'S *FLEE-ING* NOW-- AND IF THE VAMPIRE KING WILL ONLY BE GOOD ENOUGH TO *PURSUE* HIM, RATHER THAN TO *REMIND* HIM OF HIS VOW--!

AND HE *DOES!*

WAIT HERE, MY HELPLESS ONES! I CAN SCALE THESE WALLS AS EASILY AS *HE*, THOUGH THEY WERE AS SHEER AS IN SOUTH OF KUSH.

I DENIED YOU THE PLEASURE OF HIS *MEN*-- BUT I'LL GIVE YOU WHAT'S LEFT IN *HIS* BODY, RIGHT ENOUGH, WHEN I'VE FINISHED WITH IT.

THE HOWLS OF THE "MEN WHO DRINK BLOOD" ARE ALMOST MORE NAUSEOUS TO CONAN, HIGH ABOVE, THAN IS THE HOARSE WHISPER OF *K'CHAMA* HIMSELF...

FOR, HE IS *MORE* OR *LESS* THAN HUMAN, AFTER ALL... WHILE THEY ARE *MEN* LIKE HIMSELF, FOR ALL THEIR POINTED TEETH AND EARS.

WELL? *COME AHEAD*, MONSTER!

WE'LL SEE IF YOUR STRENGTH CAN OVER-COME ONE WHO HAS THE *HIGH GROUND.*

BUT SOMEHOW THE CIMMERIAN KNOWS IN HIS HEART... THAT IT QUITE POSSIB-LY *WILL.*

NO MATTER! HE'LL FIGHT. TO THE END-- AND BE PROUD TO DIE A *MAN*, NOT A THING FOREVER LOCKED OUT OF TIME.

THEN, ABRUPTLY, FROM *BELOW,* WHERE THE HUMAN DRELLIKS WAIT, THEIR EYES WIDE WITH ANTICIPATION...

GA GAA

WHO--?

THE BAMULA HAVE RETURNED!!

AND CONAN SMILES GRIMLY IN THE LAST MINUTES OF NIGHT, BEFORE THE SUN RISES, TO SEE *BASUTO* LEADING THE ATTACK.

HE DID, INDEED, KNOW HIS SOLE ARCH-RIVAL BETTER THAN BASUTO KNEW HIMSELF.

FEAR THE DRELLIKS THOUGH THE BAMULA MIGHT, HE HAD BEEN CERTAIN BASUTO WOULD *RALLY* THEM, ONCE HE GOT THEM OUT OF THE BLOOD-DRINKERS' WALLS.

RIGHT *NOW,* HOWEVER--

YOUR FOLLOWERS WILL *DIE,* DOG-- IF NOT AT ONCE, THEN WHEN THE *SUN* COMES UP IN A MOMENT--

--AND THEY BECOME TOO WEAK AND *LETHARGIC* TO FIGHT.

IT SHALL MATTER LITTLE TO *YOU,* BARBARIAN.

YOU'LL NOT BE *ALIVE* TO BEHOLD EITHER VICTORY OR DEFEAT. THIS *I* SWEAR!

"*GOOD,*" CONAN THINKS, "HE STILL HASN'T CHARGED ME ANEW WITH MY *OATH*-- AND I'LL NOT REMIND HIM OF IT!"

INSTEAD, HE BEGINS TO *CLIMB* AGAIN-- STRIVING TO KEEP OUT OF HARM'S WAY, UNTIL--

LET GO OF ME, CURSE YOU!

FOOL OF A WOMAN-SPAWNED BARBARIAN!

I COULD HAVE BROUGHT YOU LIFE UNENDING, AND ALL THE POWER THAT THAT CAN BRING.

INSTEAD, YOU CHOSE TO CLIMB AND CRAWL YOUR WAY TO AN INGLORIOUS DEATH WITHOUT WAKING--

UNNH

--AND THAT, TOO, I AM WILLING TO BRING YOU...!

WILLING-- BUT NOT ABLE, DOG!

YET, THOUGH CONAN FEELS AND HEARS THE VAMPIRE'S SKULL CRACK UNDER THE CHAIN'S BLUNT IMPACT--

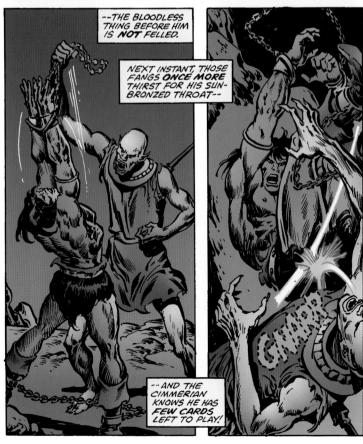

--THE BLOODLESS THING BEFORE HIM IS NOT FELLED.

NEXT INSTANT, THOSE FANGS ONCE MORE THIRST FOR HIS SUN-BRONZED THROAT--

--AND THE CIMMERIAN KNOWS HE HAS FEW CARDS LEFT TO PLAY!

FOR, HE CANNOT GO DOWN, BUT ONLY *UP*-- AND EVER, PURSUED BY A CREATURE WHICH HAS ALL THE TIME IN THIS WORLD AND THE NEXT...

I WAS A FOOL *MYSELF*, TO WISH TO SQUANDER MY MOST PRECIOUS GIFT ON YOU... SIMPLY BECAUSE YOU WERE *STRONGER* THAN OTHERS I'VE MET.

BUT, IF YOU THINK YOU CAN *CLIMB* HIGH ENOUGH TO ESCAPE ME--

--YOU ARE AS FOOLHARDY AS THE WOMAN WHO PUT THIS INEFFECTUAL *SPEAR* IN MY BACK!

SPEAR...!?

THE NEXT-- HE HAS HURLED HIMSELF INTO *SPACE*--

HA!!!!

ONE MOMENT, CONAN IS INDEED CLIMBING, THOUGH WITH NO REAL HOPE OF ESCAPE...

--BUT *NOT* INTO K'CHAMA'S IRRE-SISTIBLE TALON-EMBRACE!

WHAT--?

RATHER, IT IS THE SHAFT OF THE PROTRUDING *SPEAR* HE GRASPS IN SHEER DESPERATION...

DOLT! WHAT GOOD WILL THIS DO YOU?

I SHALL *RETURN* TO YOU, AS SOON AS I--

AND THEN, SUDDEN-LY-- THE DRELLIK *REMEMBERS*--

MOST OF THE *SPEAR* JUTTING FROM HIS BACK--

--IS OF *WOOD!*

72

FOR, CONAN HAS LEARNED THAT TRUE VAMPIRES ARE A *VARIED* LOT, AND WHILE METAL CAN KILL MANY OF THEM... HE RECALLED, JUST IN TIME, K'CHAMA'S *OWN* TALE...

...OF HOW THE *BAT-THING* THAT ATTACKED HIM DIED ONLY WHEN ITS HEART WAS PENETRATED BY A *WOODEN* SPEAR-SHAFT.

THE *MAN-*DRELLIKS BELOW, HOW-EVER, CAN PERISH IN *SEVERAL* WAYS...

...AS THEY ARE DOING, EVEN NOW.

AND CONAN MEANS TO *JOIN* THEM IN THE SLAYING, AFTER--

GIVE ME YOUR *LONG KNIFE,* MAN!

TO DIE FOREVER, A VAMPIRE'S *HEAD* MUST BE CUT OFF.

YET, EVEN KNOWING THIS, THE CIMMERIAN IS STARTLED TO SEE THE REPELLANT CREATURE STILL REACHING DEADLY *TALONS* AT HIM, EVEN WITH ITS EVIL HEART IMPALED ON WOOD.

A MOMENT MORE, HOWEVER, AND ITS TWITCHING HANDS ARE STILLED FOREVER.

BUT THEN, BEFORE CONAN CAN ENTER THE FRAY--

EESEE!? CROM! I THOUGHT YOU WERE--

...DEAD?? AYE... AND S-SO DID... K'CHAMA.

BUT... I COULD NOT... *WOULD* NOT DIE...

73

...UNLESS IT BE... WITH HIM...✲

CONAN, OBSERVING THIS LAST DISPLAY OF *LOVE* FROM ONE WHO FIRST WAS CURSED, THEN SCORNED...

...KNOWS NOT WHETHER TO ADMIRE HER... OR TO FEEL SICK TO HIS STOMACH.

PERHAPS... A LITTLE OF *EACH.*

IT IS *DAWN* AS THE VICTORIOUS BAMULA FOLLOW THEIR NORTH-BORN LEADER WESTWARD, BACK TOWARD THEIR OWN COUNTRY...

BUT, THE RISING SUN'S GLOW IS SCARCELY VISIBLE IN THE LIGHT OF THE GREAT *FIRE* WHICH CONSUMES WOODEN WALLS AND BODIES ALIKE.

I *HOPED* YOU'D COME BACK, BASUTO-- BUT WHY *DID* YOU?

WITH ME DEAD AND YOU ALIVE, YOU'D HAVE BEEN *WAR-CHIEF,* AS YOU WOULD LIKE TO BE.

IT WAS *YOU* WHO WERE FIRST TO FACE THE *DRELLIK-KING* IN COMBAT, NOT I.

I STILL WANT A *BAMULA* ON OUR WAR-THRONE, BUT I WOULD RATHER SERVE A *BRAVE* WHITE MAN THAN BECOME WAR-CHIEF *THAT* WAY.

THEN A TRUE *SUB-CHIEF* YOU SHALL BE, FROM THIS MOMENT.

AND, AS NEXT IN LINE AFTER ME, IT WOULD BE WELL IF YOU HAD A *WIFE* TO BEAR YOU BRAVE SONS, WOULD IT NOT?

YOU MEAN... *FELIDA,* YORUBO'S WIDOW?

I HAVE LONG ADMIRED HER, BUT--

WELL, I PROMISED HER A *MATE* WHEN AND IF I RETURNED FROM THE LAND OF THE DRELLIKS...

BUT, IF SHE'LL *HAVE* YOU, AS I SUSPECT SHE WILL, *YOU'LL* SUIT HER BETTER THAN I.

BESIDES, HE TRAVELS HIGH-EST... WHO TRAVELS *LIGHTEST.*

YET, EVEN SO, HE ACHES IN REMEM-BERING A SHE-PIRATE NAMED *BÊLIT*... AND A DAY WHEN THAT WAS NOT SO...!

NEXT ISSUE: THE VALE OF LOST WOMEN!

"Know, O prince, that between the years when the oceans drank Atlantis and the gleaming cities, and the rise of the sons of Aryas, there was an Age undreamed of, when shining kingdoms lay spread across the world like blue mantles beneath the stars.

"Hither came Conan, the Cimmerian, black-haired, sullen-eyed, sword, in hand, a thief, a reaver, a slayer, with gigantic melancholies and gigantic mirth, to tread the jeweled thrones of the Earth under his sandaled feet."

—*The Nemedian Chronicles.*

STAN LEE PRESENTS: **CONAN THE BARBARIAN**®

THE VALE of LOST WOMEN!

ROY THOMAS ✳ JOHN BUSCEMA & ERNIE CHAN
WRITER / EDITOR ILLUSTRATORS / INNOVATORS

JOE ROSEN
LETTERER

JIM SHOOTER CONSULTING EDITOR

ADAPTED FROM THE STORY BY
ROBERT E. HOWARD
CREATOR OF CONAN

OUTSIDE--

THE THUNDER OF THE **DRUMS** AND OF THE GREAT ELEPHANT-TUSK **HORNS** IS DEAFENING...

...AS **EBON FIGURES** LEAP AND DANCE...

...OMINOUS **SILHOUETTES** CARVED OUT OF **DARKNESS** AND LIMNED IN SHIMMERING **CRIMSON.**

YET, INSIDE--

THE CLAMOR IN **LIVIA'S EARS** SEEMS BUT A CONFUSED **MUTTERING**, DULL AND FAR AWAY AS SHE TOSSES AND TURNS IN THE GREAT HUT...

...AND STRIVES TO **FORGET** THE HORRIBLE THING SHE SAW, MERE MINUTES BEFORE.

SITTING UP AT LAST, SHE SEEMS UNAWARE OF THE **HIDEOUS CHANTS** FROM WITHOUT-- OR OF THE TORN **UNDERTUNIC** WHICH IS ALL THAT HER CAPTORS LEFT HER.

IT SEEMS **STRANGE**, NOW, THAT SO **SMALL** A WRONG SHOULD HAVE CAUSED HER SO MUCH **FRIGHT** AND **SHAME**, NOT SO VERY LONG AGO.

THEN, AT A SOUND FROM THE **HUT DOOR**...

ARE-- ARE THEY COMING FOR **ME** NOW?

THE LITHE, PANTHER-ISH **KUSHITE WOMAN**, HOWEVER, SAYS **NOTHING**...

...MERELY **SMILES** FIENDISHLY, AS SHE SETS DOWN THE BAMBOO DISH OF SMOKING MEAT, ROASTED YAMS, AND NATIVE BREAD.

SPEAK TO ME! WH-WHAT DO THEY INTEND TO **DO** WITH ME?

M-MY **BROTHER--** THEY--!

SHE CAN SAY NO MORE.

AND THE SINGLE, TAUNTING *LAUGH* HER VISITOR TOSSES BACK OVER HER SHOULDER AS SHE DEPARTS, BESPEAKS MORE *INSOLENCE* THAN ANY *CIVILIZED* WOMAN COULD HAVE SUGGESTED WITH SPOKEN INSULTS.

MECHANICALLY, LIVIA PARTAKES OF THE *FOOD*, AND THE *YARATI BEER*... WITHOUT TASTING EITHER.

STILL THE VIVIDNESS OF HER *MENTAL PICTURES* MAKE THE VISIBLE WORLD SEEM TO HER AN *UNREAL PANORAMA* OF GHOSTS AND SHADOWS.

IT IS AN ABRUPT *CHANGE* IN THE TIMBRE OF THE DRUMS AND HORNS THAT DRAWS HER TO THE *SIDE* OF THE HUT...

...TO STARE, WITHOUT CONSCIOUS THOUGHT, AT THE SHIFTING MASS OF *MEN* AND *WOMEN*, LIGHTED ONLY BY THE MOON AND THE SINGLE GREAT FIRE.

THEN, THROUGH THE BAMBOO CRACK, SHE *SEES* HIM THERE ON HIS *IVORY STOOL*--

--A SQUAT, TOAD-LIKE *SHAPE*, ABYSMAL AND REPULSIVE--

--ONLY THE APPALLING VITALITY OF HIS *EYES* BELYING THE INERT SUGGESTION OF THE *GROSS BODY*.

THIS, SHE SUDDENLY REMEMBERS, IS *BAJUJH*, KING OF THE *BAKALAH!*

AND, SEEING HIM, LIVIA'S PAIN IS *DROWNED IN HATE*-- HATE SO INTENSE IT IN TURN *BECOMES* PAIN!

SHE CAN *FEEL* HER HATRED FLOWING ALMOST *TANGIBLY* OUT ALONG THE LINE OF HER *VISION*...

YET, IF FAT *BAJUJH* FEELS ANY PSYCHIC DISCOMFORT FROM HER LOATHING, HE DOES NOT *SHOW* IT.

HE MERELY CONTINUES TO CRAM HIS FROGLIKE MOUTH TO CAPACITY WITH GREAT HANDFULS OF *FOOD*...AND TO STARE *STRAIGHT AHEAD* OF HIM.

STARE-- AT *WHAT*, LIVIA WONDERS ABSENTLY.

THEN, SHE NOTES THAT A *BROAD LANE* IS BEING FORMED BY *BAJUJH'S* SUBJECTS...

...AND VAGUELY REALIZES THAT, *DOWN* THIS LANE, SOME *IMPORTANT PERSONAGE* WILL SOON COME STRIDING.

AND-- ONE *DOES!*

TO LIVIA'S *AMAZEMENT,* HOWEVER, IT IS A *BRONZED GIANT* WHO WALKS BEFORE THE *PROUD, BLACK* FIGURES WHICH MARCH THREE ABREAST.

A *WHITE MAN*-- HERE SO FAR SOUTH EVEN OF *STYGIA!*

LIVIA FEELS THE *TENSENESS* IN THE AIR...THOUGH SHE IS ONLY DIMLY AWARE OF WHAT IT *PORTENDS.*

FOR, IT IS *NOT* IN THE MANNER OF A SUPPLICANT OR A SUBORDINATE THAT THE NEWCOMER STRIDES UP TO BAJUJH'S IVORY STOOL.

FOR A MOMENT, BAJUJH *SITS*-- CRANING HIS SHORT NECK UPWARD, LIKE THE GREAT FROG HE SO RESEMBLES.

THEN, AS IF *PULLED* AGAINST HIS WILL BY THE OTHER'S *STEADY GLARE*--

--THE KING OF THE BAKALAHS *RISES* FROM HIS CHAIR, TO STAND GROTESQUELY BOBBING HIS SHAVEN HEAD!

INSTANTLY, THE TENSION IS *BROKEN*...

...AS THE BAKALAHS SALUTE THE *STRANGERS,* AND THE LATTER IN TURN BOOM A ROYAL SALUTE TO *KING BAJUJH.*

WHOEVER THE NEWCOMER IS, LIVIA KNOWS-- EVEN IN HER PAIN AND HATRED-- THAT HE MUST BE A *POWER INDEED* IN THIS WILD LAND, IF *BAJUJH OF BAKALAH* RISES TO GREET HIM.

AND, *POWER* HERE MEANS *MILITARY PRESTIGE,* AND NAUGHT ELSE!

FOR *HOURS* SHE WATCHES, AS THE BRONZE MAN AND HIS WARRIORS *MINGLE* WITH THE BAKALAH-- DANCING, FEASTING, SWIGGING BEER.

SHE NOTES THAT, SINCE *HE* HAS NO STOOL, *BAJUJH* SITS ON THE MATS BESIDE HIM.

ALL THIS CEREMONY COURTESY POINTS TO *POWER--STRENGTH-- PRESTIGE!*

LIVIA TREMBLES WITH EXCITEMENT, AS A BREATHLESS *PLAN* BEGINS TO FORM IN HER SEETHING MIND.

GRADUALLY, THE ROAR OF REVELRY *LESSENS.*

AT LAST, EVEN *BAJUJH* STRIVES TO *RISE--*

--AND, STUMBLING, IS CAUGHT BY HIS *WARRIORS.*

THEY BEAR HIM, AS *GRACEFULLY* AS POSSIBLE, TO HIS *HUT.*

IT IS A SIGNAL, MORE OR LESS, THAT IT IS TIME FOR THE GORGING AND GUZZLING TO *END.*

THE *BRONZE MAN,* APPARENTLY NONE THE WORSE FOR WEAR, IS ESCORTED TO THE *GUEST HUT* BY SUCH OF THE BAKALAH HEADMEN AS ARE ABLE TO REEL ALONG.

HE DIS- APPEARS *INTO IT...*

79

AND LIVIA NOTICES THAT A DOZEN OF *HIS OWN SPEARMEN* TAKE THEIR PLACES AROUND IT.

EVIDENTLY, THE TALL STRANGER IS TAKING *NO CHANCES* ON BAJUJH'S PROTESTATIONS OF *FRIENDSHIP.*

SOON AFTERWARD, HER *HEART* BEATING HAMMERLIKE--

--SHE MOVES TO THE *BACK* OF HER PRISON HUT.

THE *GUARD* THERE IS *SNORING AWAY,* AS SHE HAD PRAYED HE WOULD BE.

LIKE AN *IVORY SHADOW* SHE GLIDES ACROSS THE SPACE BETWEEN THE HUTS-- TO *CRAWL* BY A BACK ROUTE BENEATH THE BRONZE MAN'S QUARTERS.

WITH LUCK, SHE FINDS A *LOOSE BOARD*-- AND PUSHES IT SLOWLY, CAREFULLY *UP* AND *IN.*

FIRELIGHT FROM OUTSIDE FAINTLY *ILLUMINES* THE INTERIOR OF THE HUT AS SHE POKES HER *HEAD* IN.

THEN--

BONES OF CROM--

WHAT HAVE WE *HERE??*

OUHH--!

IT TAKES ALL HER RESOLVE NOT TO *SHRIEK*-- NOR DOES SHE UNDERSTAND THE *ALIEN DIALECT* HE SPEAKS...

OH, *PLEASE*-- N-NOT SO *LOUD!* THEY WILL *HEAR*...!

AN *OPHIREAN,* EH?

WELL, *I* KNOW THAT TONGUE-- AT LEAST A *LITTLE*-- THOUGH I'VE HAD *SCANT USE* FOR IT THESE PAST FEW YEARS!

NOW, **WHO ARE YOU?**

BY MITRA, I NEVER THOUGHT TO FIND A **WOMAN OF OPHIR** IN THIS HELLISH LAND!

M-MY NAME IS **LIVIA**-- I AM **BAJUJH'S CAPTIVE!** I--

OH, PLEASE-- **LISTEN** TO ME! I CANNOT STAY HERE **LONG**, OR THEY WILL **MISS** ME!

TELL YOUR STORY, THEN-- FOR YOU'VE SURELY **RISKED** MUCH TO CARRY IT TO ME!

I AM-- OF THE **HOUSE OF CHELKUS**-- SCIENTISTS AND NOBLEMEN OF **OPHIR**.

MY BR-BROTHER...WAS **THETELES!**

BY SPECIAL PERMISSION OF THE **KING OF STYGIA**, HE WAS ALLOWED TO GO TO **KHESHATTA, CITY OF MAGICIANS**-- TO STUDY THEIR **ARTS**-- AND I ACCOMPANIED HIM.

HE WAS ONLY-- A **BOY**-- YOUNGER THAN MYSELF...!

THEN-- THE **BLACK KUSHITES** RAIDED KHESHATTA-- EVEN AS WE WERE **APPROACHING** THE CITY.

THEY **TOOK** US-- ONLY TO BE **CUT DOWN** IN TURN, NOT FAR FROM HERE, BY A BAND OF **BAKALAH RAIDERS!**

THIS MORNING, M-MY **BROTHER**-- HE WAS **MUTILATED**-- **BUTCHERED**-- RIGHT BEFORE MY VERY **EYES!**

THEY FED HIS **BODY** TO THE **JACKALS**, AND I-- I--

YOU SAY **NOTHING!** HOW CAN YOU SIMPLY **STAND** THERE-- LIKE A **DUMB BRUTE?**

ARE YOU BUT A **BEAST**-- LIKE THOSE **OTHERS** OUT THERE??

BEAST! BEAST! BEAST!

THE BRONZE MAN HEEDS LIVIA'S **FISTS** NO MORE THAN HE MIGHT THE BUZZING OF A **FLY**...

...AND SHE **SINKS** TO THE FLOOR.

YOU ARE A **BARBARIAN**-- AN **ANIMAL**-- JUST AS **THEY** ARE!

YOU HAVE **NO HONOR**-- BUT ONLY A **PRICE**, LIKE EVERYONE ELSE!

WELL, I WILL **GIVE** YOU A **PRICE!**

AM I NOT **FAIR?** A WORTHY **REWARD** FOR BLOODLETTING?

KILL BAJUJH-- AND I WILL BE YOUR **SLAVE!**

81

FOR AN INSTANT, THE BRONZED GIANT MERELY **LOOMS** OVER HER, LIKE SOME COLOSSAL, BROODING FIGURE OF **SLAUGHTER AND DESTRUCTION,** FINGERING THE HILT OF HIS BLADE. THEN...

YOU SPEAK AS IF YOU WERE **FREE** TO GIVE YOURSELF AT YOUR **PLEASURE**... AS IF THE GIFT OF YOURSELF HAD THE POWER TO SWING **KINGDOMS.**

WHY SHOULD I **KILL** BAJUJH TO OBTAIN YOU?

WOMEN ARE **CHEAP** IN THIS LAND.

IF I WANTED YOU, BAJUJH WOULD **GIVE** YOU TO ME, RATHER THAN **FIGHT** ME!

AND LIVIA IS **SPEECHLESS,** KNOWING HIS WORDS ARE **TRUE.**

YOU SAID I WAS A **BARBARIAN**-- BE THANKFUL THAT I **AM!**

I AM **CONAN,** A **CIMMERIAN**-- AND I LIVE BY THE **SWORD'S EDGE.**

I'LL **NOT** LEAVE A HIGH-BORN WOMAN IN THE CLUTCHES OF A **SAVAGE**...

...NOR WOULD I **EVER** TAKE A WOMAN AGAINST HER **WILL!**

THEN-- YOU'LL **HELP** ME?

AYE-- FOR MY **OWN** REASONS.

I CAME HERE AT **BAJUJH'S REQUEST**-- HE WANTS ME TO JOIN HIM IN AN **ATTACK** ON JIHIJI.

TONIGHT WE **FEASTED;** TOMORROW WE'LL HOLD **COUNCIL.**

HE'D TURN ON **ME,** AFTER WE'D LOOTED JIHIJI TOGETHER-- SO I'LL GET HIM **FIRST.**

I'VE NOT FOUGHT MY WAY TO BEING **WAR-CHIEF OF THE BAMULA** WITH-OUT LEARNING **THAT** MUCH WISDOM.

BAJUJH'S **TOO DRUNK** TO BOTHER YOU TONIGHT...

...SO GET BACK TO YOUR HUT AND **SLEEP,** KNOWING IT IS NOT FOR **BAJUJH** BUT FOR **CONAN** THAT YOU PRESERVE YOUR BEAUTY!

WITH MINGLED EMOTIONS, LIVIA MAKES HER WAY **BACK,** UNSEEN.

ALL THE NEXT DAY, CONAN SITS IN THE **HUT OF BAJUJH**-- AND SHE CANNOT KNOW WHAT PASSES BETWEEN THEM.

THEN, **NIGHT** FALLS AGAIN-- AND ONCE MORE THE TWO CHIEFS SQUAT DOWN TO **FEAST** AND TO HOLD A FINAL, CEREMONIAL **COUNCIL.**

THIS TIME, THERE IS CONSIDERABLY **LESS** BEER-GUZZLING.

LIVIA OBSERVES THE *BAMULAS*-- THOSE PROUD, TALL EBON WARRIORS WHOM CONAN *LEADS*--

--SEES THEM *CONVERGING*, WITH A SEEMING *CASUALNESS*, UPON THE *CIRCLE* WHERE HE AND BAJUJH SIT.

THEN, AS SHE WATCHES THE BARBARIAN GNAW A GREAT *BEEF BONE*, SHE NOTICES HIM CASTING A QUICK *GLANCE* ACROSS HIS SHOULDER.

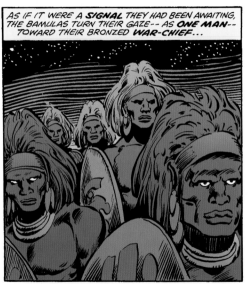

AS IF IT WERE A *SIGNAL* THEY HAD BEEN AWAITING, THE BAMULAS TURN THEIR GAZE-- AS *ONE MAN*-- TOWARD THEIR BRONZED *WAR-CHIEF*...

NEXT INSTANT, QUICK AS A SPRING WOLF, CONAN *STRIKES*-- DEALING BAJUJH'S *OWN* WAR-CHIEF A *MORTAL BLOW* WITH THE HEAVY *BONE*!

EVEN AS LIVIA HEARS THE *CRUNCHING* OF HIS SKULL BENEATH THE *IMPACT*--

--A *FRIGHTFUL YELL* RENDS THE NIGHT SKIES-- AS THE BAMULAS GO INTO ACTION LIKE *BLOOD-MAD PANTHERS*!

YEE YEE YEE YEE

WITHIN MOMENTS, BAKALAH IS A *MADHOUSE* THAT SWIFTLY REDDENS INTO A *SHAMBLES*!

THE BAKALAH HAD *EXPECTED* THE TRUCE TO BE BROKEN, YES--

--BUT BY *THEMSELVES*, AT A TIME AND PLACE OF *BAJUJH'S CHOOSING*!

UNHAPPY THE TRICKSTER WHO DELAYS HIS OWN SOLE TRICK *TOO LONG*!

FROM HIDING, LIVIA CROUCHES FROZEN-- THE YELLS OF *PAIN* AND *FURY* SMITING HER TORTURED NERVES LIKE A *PHYSICAL IMPACT*--

--AS *WRITHING*, *SLASHING* FORMS BLUR BEFORE HER--

--ONLY TO *SPRING OUT* AGAIN WITH HORRIFYING *DISTINCTNESS*.

SHE SEES *CONAN*--THE ONLY BRONZED FORM AMONG SO MANY DARKER ONES--

--PLUNGE *SWORD-FIRST* INTO A STRUGGLING *KNOT OF MEN* ABOUT A SCARLET *FIRE* RAGING OUT OF CONTROL--

--AND SHE GLIMPSES A *FAT SQUAT SHAPE* TREMBLING IN ITS *MIDST*!

PLOWING THROUGH, THE CIMMERIAN IS NOW *VISIBLE*, NOW *HIDDEN* FROM VIEW AS HIS BROAD *BLADE* FLASHES...

THEN, SUDDENLY, THE OPHIREAN UTTERS A SHRILL, INARTICULATE *CRY*--WHICH EVEN *SHE* CAN SCARCELY HEAR ABOVE THE *DIN* WITHOUT--

--AS SHE BEHOLDS *CONAN'S* TALL FORM, STRIDING TOWARD HER *HUT*--

--AND, IN HIS HAND, A *RELIC* SHE CAN IDENTIFY, EVEN THOUGH IT IS HIDDEN IN *SHADOWS!*

NNOOO!!

THE BARBARIAN HAS *PAID THE PRICE*-- AND IS COMING TO *CLAIM* HER--

--BEARING THE *AWFUL TOKEN* OF HIS PAYMENT!

DELIRIOUS NOW WITH *FEAR* OF HIM, SHE FLEES BY SOME OBSCURE INSTINCT TOWARD THE *CORRAL*--

--JUST AS A *BAMULA WARRIOR* IS RELEASING THE HORSES TO ADD TO THE *BAKALAH CONFUSION!*

EVEN *HE* CANNOT STOP HER AS SHE GRASPS BLINDLY AT THE FLYING MANE OF A RACING *MARE*--

-- AND *CLINGS* THERE DESPERATELY TO THE BACK OF A *BEAST* THAT RACES LIKE THE *WIND!*

LIVIA CANNOT *GUIDE* THE STEED-- NOR DOES SHE *TRY* TO, IN THIS WILD MOMENT.

IT IS ENOUGH THAT THE *YELLS* AND THE GLOW OF THE *FIRE* ARE FADING OUT BEHIND HER...

SHE IS AWARE ONLY OF A DAZED NEED TO *HOLD* TO THE FLOWING MANE--

--AND RIDE, *RIDE*-- OVER THE RIM OF THE WORLD AND *AWAY* FROM ALL AGONY AND GRIEF AND HORROR!

FOR **HOURS** THE WIRY STEED RACES, DRIVEN ON BY SOME **ANIMAL FEAR** ALL ITS OWN.

THEN, ABRUPTLY, TOPPING A STARLIT **CREST**--

--IT **STUMBLES**, HURLING ITS RIDER **HEADLONG!**

OHHH

RISING ON THE SOFT, CUSHIONING **SWARD**, LIVIA BEHOLDS HER **MOUNT** TROTTING AWAY.

AND, AS SHE RISES, SHE ALSO NOTICES... THE **SILENCE**.

AFTER THE **DEATH-CLAMOR** AT THE BAKALAH VILLAGE, SHE IS SUDDENLY **GLAD** OF THE MOONLESS NIGHT... AND OF HER OWN **ALONENESS**.

A **BROAD VALLEY** LIES BEFORE HER, WHERE **GREAT WHITE BLOSSOMS** WAVE SCATTERED IN THE STARLIGHT...

AND SHE MOVES **TOWARD** THEM, EVEN AS THE SIGHT OF THEM GIVES RISE IN HER TO A **VAGUE MEMORY** SHE CANNOT QUITE PLACE.

SHE REMEMBERS DIMLY THAT THE **BLACKS** SPOKE OF THAT VALLEY **SHUNNING** IT, AND CALLING IT THE **VALE OF LOST WOMEN**...

NOW, ABRUPTLY, SHE RECALLS **WHY**--

--AS SHE SEES **FIGURES** STEALING FROM THE DENSER SHADOWS, LIKE CREATURES OF A **DREAM**--

86

--LITHE, BROWN-SKINNED **WOMEN**, WITH **PALE BLOSSOMS** ON THEIR NIGHT-BLACK HAIR.

THEY DO NOT **SPEAK**...

...AND THEIR EYES ARE **LUMINOUS**, RADIANT IN THE STARSHINE-- BUT THEY ARE NOT **HUMAN** EYES!

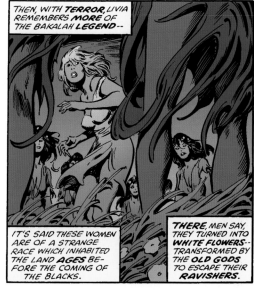

THEN, WITH **TERROR**, LIVIA REMEMBERS **MORE** OF THE BAKALAH **LEGEND**--

IT'S SAID THESE WOMEN ARE OF A STRANGE RACE WHICH INHABITED THE LAND **AGES** BEFORE THE COMING OF THE BLACKS.

THERE, MEN SAY, THEY TURNED INTO **WHITE FLOWERS**-- TRANSFORMED BY THE **OLD GODS** TO ESCAPE THEIR **RAVISHERS**.

YET, EVEN AS **FEAR** DESCENDS ON HER IN A WAVE, THE OPHIREAN IS **SEIZED** BY THOSE STRONG YET SOFT HANDS--

PLEASE-- LET ME **GO!**

I-- I MEAN YOU **NO HARM**--!

AT THEIR EERIE TOUCH, LIVIA FEELS **COLDNESS** RUNNING THROUGH HER VEINS-- HER LIMBS TURN **BRITTLE**--

AND, LIKE AN **IVORY STATUE**, INCAPABLE OF SPEECH OR MOVEMENT, SHE IS **LIFTED**-- CARRIED ACROSS THE SWARD--

--LAID UPON A **WORN ALTAR-STONE** SHE HAD NOT SEEN BEFORE-- AMID A **BED OF FLOWERS!**

THE WOMEN **DANCE** SUPPLELY--

--AS A **LOW CHANT** ARISES FROM THEIR LIPS--

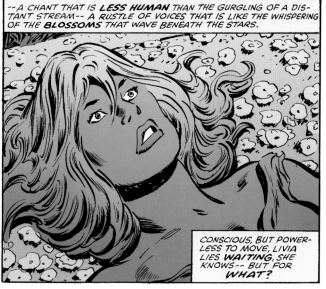

--A CHANT THAT IS **LESS HUMAN** THAN THE GURGLING OF A DISTANT STREAM-- A RUSTLE OF VOICES THAT IS LIKE THE WHISPERING OF THE **BLOSSOMS** THAT WAVE BENEATH THE STARS.

CONSCIOUS, BUT POWERLESS TO MOVE, LIVIA LIES **WAITING**, SHE KNOWS-- BUT FOR **WHAT?**

THEN, *HIGH ABOVE*, she sees a *BLACK DOT* AGAINST THE STARS... GROWING *LARGER* AS IT DRAWS LOWER, *NEARER*.

THE *WOMEN'S CHANTING* RISES HIGHER, TO A SOFT PAEAN OF *SOUL-LESS JOY*, AS THE THING ABOVE DROPS DOWN ON *GREAT, BATLIKE WINGS*--

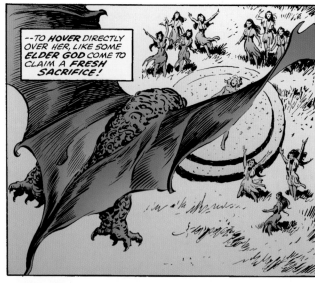

--TO *HOVER* DIRECTLY OVER HER, LIKE SOME *ELDER GOD* COME TO CLAIM A *FRESH SACRIFICE!*

AND, AS SHE LOOKS UPON THAT *ULTIMATE HORROR*, BORN IN NIGHT-BLACK *GULFS* BEYOND THE REACH OF *A MADMAN'S WILDEST DREAMS*-- SHE MANAGES TO *SCREAM*--!

AAIEEEE

SHE SCARCELY *COMPREHENDS* AS HER CRY IS ANSWERED BY A DEEP, MENACING *SHOUT*...

L'IVIA!

--OR BY THE POUNDING OF *RUSHING FEET*.

SHE ONLY KNOWS THAT THERE IS A SUDDEN *SWIRL*, AS OF SWIFT WATERS-- AND THEN THE BROWN WOMEN ARE *GONE*--

--AND *OVER* HER, 'TWIXT HER OWN BODY AND THE *BLACK SHADOW*, IS--

CONAN--?!

88

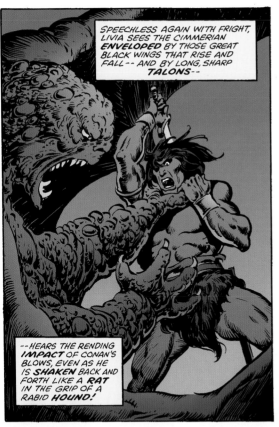

SPEECHLESS AGAIN WITH FRIGHT, LIVIA SEES THE CIMMERIAN **ENVELOPED** BY THOSE GREAT BLACK WINGS THAT RISE AND FALL -- AND BY LONG, SHARP **TALONS**--

--HEARS THE RENDING **IMPACT** OF CONAN'S BLOWS, EVEN AS HE IS **SHAKEN** BACK AND FORTH LIKE A **RAT** IN THE GRIP OF A RABID **HOUND**!

SHE **WITNESSES** THE DEVILISH BATTLE AS IN A **NIGHTMARE**--

--BEHOLDS THE DARK THING **WAVER** AND **STAGGER** IN MID-AIR, AS IT ATTEMPTS TO **WING SKY-WARD** WITH ITS WRITHING **HUMAN BURDEN**!

THEN, A POWERFUL **KICK** FROM THE BARBARIAN--

--AND **BOTH** FALL TO-GETHER TO THE **SWARD**--

--THE **BLOOD** OF EACH MING-LING WITH THE WEIRD **WHITE PETALS** THAT LIE STREWN LIKE A CARPET!

NOW, SHE SEES CONAN TEAR HIMSELF **FREE** FOR AN INSTANT TO RAISE HIS BROADSWORD ABOVE HIS HEAD LIKE AN **EXECUTIONER'S AXE**--

--AND BRING IT SOLIDLY **DOWN** AGAIN!

THE MONSTER IS TOO STRONG WITH UN-EARTHLY LIFE TO BE SLAIN, EVEN BY SUCH A BLOW--

THUS, NEXT MO-MENT, THERE IS A THRESHING BEAT OF **CRIPPLED WINGS** AS IT TEARS **CLEAR**--

--TO SOAR UPWARD AND **VANISH** AMONG THE MULTITUDE OF **STARS!**

BELOW, ITS **CONQUEROR** STAGGERS DIZZILY--**AMAZED** AT VICTORY, YET READY TO **RENEW** THE GHASTLY BATTLE.

BUT, WHEN THE CREATURE DOES **NOT** RETURN, HE TURNS TO THE **ALTAR**...

H-HOW DID YOU--?

MY **MEN** SAW YOU RIDE OUT OF THE **VILLAGE.**

I **FOLLOWED** YOU AS BEST I COULD, THOUGH THEY WOULDN'T COME **WITH** ME, AND--

WHAT'S **WRONG**, GIRL? YOU **RECOIL** FROM ME-- AS IF **I** WERE THAT **DEMON-BAT** COME TO CLAIM YOU!

I-- I **SAW** YOU-- **KILL** BAJUJH--

I-- SAW HIS **HEAD!** YOU--

WELL, WHAT IF I **DID?**

HE'D HAVE DONE THE SAME TO **ME,** ONE DAY.

CROM, YOU CIVILIZED **PEOPLE!** YOU **BEGGED** ME TO SLAY HIM-- AND NOW YOU **REVILE** ME THAT I **DID!**

AND AFTER THE TROUBLE I HAD **TRACKING** YOU BY STARLIGHT!

WHAT **VALE OF DEVILS** IS THIS, ANYWAY?

WHAT **WAS** THAT THING?

THE BAKALAH CALLED IT A *GOD*-- FROM FAR AWAY AND *LONG AGO!*

A DEVIL FROM THE *OUTER DARK*, EH? WELL, THEY'RE NOT *UN-COMMON.*

THEY LURK AS *THICK AS FLEAS* OUTSIDE THE *BELT OF LIGHT* WHICH SURROUNDS THIS WORLD.

I'VE HEARD THE *WISE MEN OF ZAMORA* TALK OF THEM.

SOME FEW FIND THEIR WAY TO *EARTH*-- BUT WHEN THEY DO, THEY MUST TAKE ON *FLESH* OF SOME SORT, WHICH MAKES THEM *VULNERABLE.*

COME! MY MEN AWAIT ME BEYOND THAT *RIDGE* OF-- *NOW* WHAT'S WRONG?

I--*RAN AWAY* FROM YOU, CIMMERIAN!

I WAS *YOURS* BY THE BARGAIN WE MADE-- BUT I'D HAVE *FLED* YOU, IF I COULD.

YET, YOU FOLLOWED ME-- *SAVED* ME--!

OH, DON'T *COWER* THERE LIKE A SCOLDED *PUPPY*, LIVIA!

IT WAS A *FOUL* BARGAIN I MADE-- I DECIDED THAT ON THE WAY *HERE.*

THE WAYS OF MEN *VARY* IN DIFFERENT LANDS-- BUT A MAN NEED NOT BE A *SWINE*, WHEREVER HE IS.

I DON'T REGRET *KILL-ING BAJUJH*-- BUT YOU'RE NO WENCH TO BE *BOUGHT* AND *SOLD.*

BESIDES, YOU'RE *NOT TOUGH ENOUGH* FOR THIS LAND-- YOU'D NOT *LAST* LONG, FOLLOWING THE LIFE I *THRIVE* ON.

I'LL TAKE YOU AS FAR AS THE *STYGIAN BORDER*, WHENCE YOU CAN BE SENT *HOME.*

HOME? TO *OPHIR...?*

TEARS WELL SUDDENLY IN LIVIA'S EYES, AND...

CROM, GIRL! DON'T *DO* THAT!

YOU'D THINK I WAS DOING YOU A *FAVOR* IN KICKING YOU OUT OF THIS COUNTRY!

HAVEN'T I *EXPLAINED* TO YOU THAT YOU'RE JUST *NOT* THE PROPER *WOMAN* FOR THE *WAR-CHIEF OF THE BAMULA?*

NEXT: *CASTLE OF* WHISPERING SHADOWS!

Stan Lee PRESENTS: CONAN THE BARBARIAN®

WHISPERING SHADOWS!

ADAPTED FROM THE STORY "CASTLE OF TERROR" BY
L. SPRAGUE DE CAMP & LIN CARTER

FEATURING THE HERO CREATED BY
ROBERT E. HOWARD

THE SCENE IS AS *REAL* TO CONAN OF CIMMERIA AS IF IT WERE HAPPENING AT THIS VERY MOMENT--

THE *HIGH PRIEST OF AJUJO*, THAT SAVAGE GOD'S EMISSARY AMONG THE BAMULA, WAVES A GRIMLY ACCUSING FINGER AT THE WHITE *WAR-CHIEF* OF THAT FIERCE PEOPLE...

IT IS THIS *PALE-SKINNED DOG* WHO HAS BROUGHT AJUJO'S ANGER UPON THE BAMULA!

KILL HIM-- AND THE GOD WILL LOOK WITH *FAVOR* ONCE MORE UPON OUR TRIBE!

AND CONAN, ONLY LATELY CALLED AMRA THE LION, STARES BACK IN SOMBRE, NONCOMMITTAL *SILENCE.*

ONE FALSE OR TIMID MOVE, HE KNOWS, AND THE SUPERSTITIOUS BAMULA WILL *FALL* UPON HIM, AT THEIR WITCH-DOCTOR'S COMMAND...

...AND *HIS* HEAD WILL JOIN THOSE SKULLS ALREADY IMPALED ON STAKES BY THE VILLAGE GATE...!

LG
578

| ROY THOMAS WRITER/EDITOR | JOHN BUSCEMA & ERNIE CHAN ILLUSTRATORS |
| JOE ROSEN, LETTERER | JIM SHOOTER CONSULTING EDITOR |

WELL? WHAT HAVE YOU TO SAY TO *AJUJO'S CHARGES*?

THEY ARE *YOUR* CHARGES, WITCH-MAN, NOT AJUJO'S... SO I WILL NOT ANSWER THEM.

LISTEN, THEN-- YOU TOO, MEN OF THE BAMULA-- AND KNOW WHY YOU SHOULD *SLAY* THIS MAN--!

"*LONG MONTHS AGO* HE CAME AMONG US--BECOMING WAR-CHIEF AND POISONING YOUR MINDS AGAINST AJUJO'S APPOINTED PRIESTS.

"HE DID NOT THEN HIDE HIS *CONTEMPT* FOR OUR GODS--AND EVEN ABOLISHED THE *HUMAN BLOOD SACRIFICE* SO SACRED TO AJUJO.

"NOW, OF LATE, A PERIOD OF UNBROKEN *DROUGHT* HAS COME UPON THE JUNGLE.

"RIVERS HAVE SHRUNK... WATER-HOLES HAVE DRIED UP.

"*WAR* HAS SWEPT THE LAND ON THE HEELS OF DROUGHT AND FAMINE... NOR HAVE THE BAMULA ALWAYS *WON* THEIR BATTLES FOR WATER...

"...AS THEY SURELY WOULD HAVE, WERE OUR NEGLECTED GODS NOT *ANGRY* WITH US.

"INSTEAD, SOME OF OUR OUTER VILLAGES HAVE GONE UP IN *FLAMES*... WHOLE CLANS BEEN SLAUGHTERED.

"CONAN SPEAKS OF PREPARATION, OF STRATEGY... BUT IT IS *AJUJO'S WRATH* WHICH SPEAKS LOUDEST.

"AND NOW, *PLAGUE* HAS COME INTO THE LAND.

"BE NOT DECEIVED BY HIS TALK OF *WEAKNESS* CAUSED BY DROUGHT AND FAMINE, MEN OF THE BAMULA!

"YOUR SOLE WEAKNESS IS HAVING THIS *WHITE JACKAL* AS YOUR *WAR-CHIEF!*"

REMEMBER EVEN HOW, SOME TIME AGO, HE MADE US RETURN THE CAPTIVE *WHITE GIRL* TO THE BORDERS OF STYGIA, INSTEAD OF KEEPING HER AS A *SLAVE!**

I SAY, LET US *FLAY* THIS OUTSIDER ALIVE, AND FEED HIS HEART TO OUR *DOGS,* BEFORE--

*LAST ISSUE. --ROY.

AAAAA

I'VE HEARD *ENOUGH,* WITCH-MAN!

HE HAS *SLAIN* AJUJO'S PRIEST! *KILL HIM!*

THE IMAGES *CASCADE* NOW, ONE HARD UPON ANOTHER...

FIRST, HOW HE *TOPPLED* THE BAMULA'S BLOODSTAINED WOODEN IDOL UPON THE OTHER SHAMANS AND WARRIORS ALIKE...

...TO *FLEE,* ARMED ONLY WITH SWORD AND BOW, INTO THE DARKNESS OF THE SURROUNDING JUNGLE.

THEN, HOW FOR MANY WEARY LEAGUES HE GROPED HIS WAY *NORTHWARD,* CURSING HIMSELF ALL THE WHILE FOR NOT HAVING EXECUTED ALL THE WITCH-DOCTORS THE DAY HE TOOK COMMAND AS WAR-CHIEF.

AT LAST, HOW HE REACHED THE REGION WHERE THE CROWD-ING FOREST THINS OUT, GIVING WAY TO THE *OPEN GRASSLANDS.*

FOR, HE MEANT TO CROSS THE SAVANNA ON FOOT TO REACH THE *SEMI-CIVILIZED* KINGDOM CALLED *KUSH*--

--WHERE HIS BARBARIC STRENGTH AND SWIFT SWORD MIGHT FIND HIM EMPLOYMENT IN THE SERVICE OF THE DUSKY *TWIN MONARCHS* OF THAT ANCIENT LAND.

THERE WAS **WATER** ON THE SAVANNA... WATER ENOUGH TO MAKE HIM NEARLY FORGET THE DAMNABLE **DROUGHT** WHICH HELPED BRING HIM LOW IN THE LAND FROM WHICH HE FLED.

THERE WAS **FOOD,** TOO, FOR ONE SKILLED ENOUGH WITH A BOW AND ARROW TO BRING IT DOWN.

CONAN WAS SKILLED ENOUGH.

ALL THESE THINGS HE NOW REMEMBERS, AS IF THEY WERE THE EVENTS OF A FEW PASSING **MOMENTS,** INSTEAD OF THE CULMINATION OF LONG DAYS AND NIGHTS SINCE HE LEFT THE COUNTRY OF THE **BAMULA...**

...ONLY TO FIND HIS THOUGHTS ABRUPTLY SNATCHED AWAY FROM THE CONTEMPLATION OF THE **PAST...**

...BY A THRILL OF **PRESENT DANGER!**

SOME PRIMAL INSTINCT OF SURVIVAL ALERTS HIM TO THE **NEARNESS OF PERIL.**

HIS NAPE-HAIRS BRISTLING WITH THE TOUCH OF **UNSEEN MENACE,** THE GIANT BARBARIAN PROBES THE AIR WITH SENSITIVE NOSTRILS, SMOLDERING EYES.

NOTHING! NOTHING... AND YET--

SUDDENLY, FEELING THE FEATHERY TOUCH OF INVISIBLE EYES, HE **WHIRLS--**

--TO GLIMPSE A PAIR OF **LARGE, BLAZING ORBS** GLOWING IN THE TWILIGHT GLOOM!

NEXT INSTANT, THEY **VANISH--** BUT NOW HE KNOWS THAT **TAWNY, SINUOUS FORMS** GLIDE AFTER HIM ON SILENT FEET.

THE **LIONS OF KUSH** ARE ON HIS TRACK, LUSTING FOR HOT BLOOD AND NEW FLESH!

AN HOUR LATER, *NIGHT* HAS FALLEN OVER THE SAVANNA, SAVE FOR A NARROW BAND OF SUNSET GLOW TO HIS LEFT.

TWICE ALREADY, DESPITE THE GATHERING DARK, CONAN HAS MANAGED TO DRIVE THE LIONS OFF WITH THE FLYING DEATH OF HIS *ARROWS.*

BUT, MINUTE BY MINUTE, IT WILL GET MORE DIFFICULT TO *AIM* HIS SHAFTS WELL ENOUGH...

AND THE PRIDE OF LIONS FOLLOWING HIM, AS IF SENSING THE FACT, MOVE EVER *CLOSER.*

NOW, WITHOUT WARNING, A PAIR OF *LIONESSES* MAKE THEIR MOVE...

RRRRRR

CONAN'S ARROWS ARE STILL HIS ONLY CHANCE-- FOR, THOUGH HE IS PERHAPS THE *STRONGEST* MAN OF HIS TIME--

--ONCE A *LION* GETS HIS CLAWS AND TEETH INTO HIM, THAT STRENGTH WILL BE NO MORE EFFECTIVE THAN THAT OF A *SMALL CHILD!*

BUT PERHAPS THIS IS *NOT* THAT TIME, CONAN THINKS-- AS THE FIRST OF HIS ARROWS FINDS ITS MARK.

GRARRR

THE *SECOND* OF THE FEMALES, HOWEVER, STILL COMES ONWARD, LIKE ORANGE LIGHTNING--

ALL RIGHT, CAT--

--THIS IS FOR *YOU!*

HRR RK

WHETHER HE HAS SLAIN OR ONLY WOUNDED THE PREDATORS, HOWEVER, HE CANNOT KNOW...

NOR IS HE UNAWARE THAT THERE ARE *EIGHT* OR *TEN MORE*, INVISIBLE IN THE DARKNESS AND TALL GRASS.

COME OUT, DAMN YOU-- WHERE I CAN PUT A *SHAFT* BETWEEN YOUR GREEN EYES!

BUT HIS ONLY ANSWER IS A LOW, SINISTER RUMBLE.

NOW, HE BEGINS TO *RUN*...RUN WITH A LONG, LOPING STRIDE THAT EATS UP THE LEAGUES.

ONLY HALF BELIEVING AT BEST, HE PRAYS TO HIS SAVAGE GODS FOR THE *MOON* TO EMERGE FROM THE DENSE, STORMY *CLOUDS* THAT VEIL MOST OF THE SKY.

BUT THE GODS HEAR NOT.

FOR AN *HOUR* HE RUNS...TILL HE HAS REACHED NEARLY THE LIMITS OF EVEN *HIS* IRON ENDURANCE.

AND BEHIND HIM STILL COME THE *LIONS*, WHOSE STRONG REEK AND PANTING BREATH-SOUNDS DRIFT TO HIM.

IF ONLY HE COULD *SEE* THEM--!

THEN, SUDDENLY, THE ROUND SILVER EYE OF THE *MOON* GLARES DOWN UPON THE BROAD, PLAINS...

...FLOODING THE LAND WITH *LIGHT!*

AT THAT MOMENT, THE *OLDEST MALE* OF THE PRIDE BEGINS HIS CHARGE, WITH AN EARTH-SHUDDERING *ROAR*...

G RA RR

...AND CONAN KNOWS THAT THE YOUNGER MALES AND SWIFTER LION-ESSES WILL NOT BE FAR BEHIND!

THEN, ABRUPTLY -- THE KING OF BEASTS STOPS IN *MID-CHARGE* --!

RRRRR

WELL? WHAT ARE YOU *WAITING* FOR, LONGMANE?

DECIDE TO LET YOUR *CUBS* AND *LIONESSES* DO YOUR BLOODY WORK FOR YOU, AS USUAL?

YET, EVEN AS HE HURLS HIS DEFIANCE, CONAN KNOWS THAT IS *NOT* THE ANSWER...

FOR, HE SEES TO HIS ASTONISHMENT THAT THE *ENTIRE PRIDE* HAS HALTED -- AS IF AT SOME *INVISIBLE BARRIER* --

-- ON ONE SIDE OF WHICH GROW THICK, LUSH *GRASSES* --

-- WHILE BEYOND IT, WHERE HE STANDS, THE GRASS BECOMES THIN, STUBBLY, WITH BROAD PATCHES OF *BARE EARTH.*

RRRR

A LONG MOMENT HE PAUSES THERE, FACING THE LIONS, BOW IN HAND -- WONDERING IF THEY WILL *RESUME* THEIR DEADLY CHARGE.

BUT THE GREAT CATS STAY WHERE THEY *ARE* -- GROWLING AND ROARING FROM FOAM-DRIPPING JAWS.

THEN, GETTING HIS SECOND WIND, HE PRESSES ONWARD.

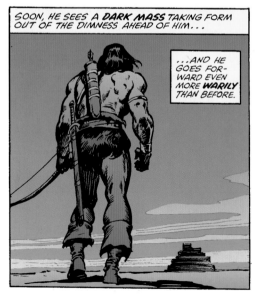

SOON, HE SEES A *DARK MASS* TAKING FORM OUT OF THE DIMNESS AHEAD OF HIM...

...AND HE GOES FORWARD EVEN MORE *WARILY* THAN BEFORE.

AT LENGTH, HE SEES IT FOR WHAT IT IS --

A HUGE *CASTLE* OR *FORTRESS* OF SOME SORT -- MADE OF DENSE BLACK STONE AND LYING PARTLY IN *RUINS.*

WHAT IN CROM'S NAME --?

YOU **BOTHER** ME, CASTLE -- WITH ODD ANGLES IN YOUR ARCHES, AS IF SOMEONE **NOT QUITE SANE** HAD BUILT YOU.

BUT, IT SEEMS THERE'S A **THUNDERSTORM** BREWING ON THE SAVANNA--

--AND, AS THE SAILORS OF ARGOS SAY, **ALL** HARBORS LOOK EQUALLY SAFE DURING A **GALE.**

YET, DESPITE HIS BRAVE WORDS, CONAN'S HACKLES RISE IN SUPERSTITIOUS **AWE** AS HE STRIDES THROUGH THE DARK, WIDE PORTAL...

...TO ENTER A HIGH-VAULTED, ENORMOUS **HALL**, WHERE NOTHING SEEMS TO LIVE -- AND WHERE DUST AND DEAD LEAVES LITTER THE CRUMBLING BLACK ONYX.

THE CITADEL IS OF STAGGERING SIZE, EVEN TO ONE WHO HAS SEEN THE TEMPLE OF ZAMORA'S SPIDER-GOD AT **YEZUD** AND KING YILDIZ'S PALACE IN **TURAN.**

ITS ANTIQUITY IS BEYOND GUESSING...

BUT, IT IS THE STRANGE, BALUSTRATED **BALCONY** WHICH RUNS ABOUT THE HALL, OVER HIS HEAD, WHICH EXCITES HIS ATTENTION.

STRIVING TO REACH IT, HE ROAMS THE **CORRIDORS**, WHICH WIND AS SINUOUSLY AS A SERPENT'S TRACK.

SOME ARE WIDE AND LOW -- OTHERS, SO NARROW HE CAN SCARCELY PASS THROUGH THEM.

THEN, AT LAST--

A STAIRWAY--!

HIS UNEASY FEARS RETURN, HOWEVER -- WHEN HE REALIZES THAT THE STEPS ARE MUCH BROADER AND SHALLOWER THAN WOULD BE REQUIRED... FOR **HUMAN** FEET.

FOR A TIME LONGER, CONAN WANDERS AMID THE CARVED, COILING **ARABESQUES**...AND A MUSKY, OPHIDIAN **ODOR**.

HE FEELS ALMOST AS IF THEY ARE TRYING TO **EN-TRAP HIS MIND**...AND AT LENGTH, HE SLUMPS DOWN THERE UPON THE BALCONY...

...WHERE HE FALLS **ASLEEP**, HEARING THE BRIEF PATTER OF RAINDROPS ABOVE AS THE FIRST THUNDERSTORM MISSES THE CASTLE...

...AND MUSING, FOR SOME UNKNOWN REASON, OF THE FABLED **SERPENT-MEN OF VALUSIA**, DESTROYED IN THE LONG-AGO DAYS OF THE MAN-LEGEND **KING KULL**.

YET, EVEN AS HE SLEEPS, HIS SPIRIT-- OR **KA**, AS THE STYGIANS CALL IT-- IS AWAKE AND WATCHFUL.

THAT KA SEES DRIFTING, OMINOUS **SHADOWS** WHICH HE KNOWS, SOME-HOW, ARE **GHOSTS**...

...GHOSTS OF THOUSANDS OF **SENTIENT BEINGS**, HUMAN OR OTHER, THAT DIED WITHIN THIS AGE-OLD EDIFICE.

MORE THAN ONCE HE WAKES-- AND THEY VANISH-- AND AT LAST HE FALLS MORE **DEEPLY** ASLEEP, A MUTTERED AND WEARY **CURSE** ON HIS LIPS...

CROM DAMN... ALL SHADOWS... TO HELL...

HIS SPIRIT, STILL WATCHING IT ALL, KNOWS THAT THESE WHISPERING SHADOWS HUNGER FOR THE **BLOOD** OF THE LIVING-- FOR **CONAN'S BLOOD**.

YET, THOUGH HIS BODY LIES IN ENSORCELLED SLUMBER, THE MALEVO-LENT GHOSTS CANNOT HARM A **LIVING BEING**--

--NOT UNLESS THEY FIRST MANIFEST THEM-SELVES IN **MATERIAL FORM** ON THE PHYSICAL PLANE--

-- SOMETHING WHICH, IN THEIR **UNHOLY HUNGER**, THEY NOW BEGIN TO DO.

EACH SPIRIT ALONE IS **TOO WEAK** TO BECOME PHYSICAL, **REAL**. AH, BUT IF ALL WERE TO MERGE **TOGETHER** --!

GRADUALLY, A **HORRIFYING SHAPE**, FED BY THE LIFE-FORCE OF TEN THOUSAND GHOSTS, BEGINS TO MATERIALIZE OUT OF THE SWIRLING CLOUD OF SHADOWS...

...WHILE CONAN, DEEP IN HIS MYSTIC TRANCE, SLEEPS ON.

JUST THEN, **THUNDER** CRASHES DEAFENINGLY ABOVE THE BARREN LANDSCAPE OUTSIDE...

...THE SULFUROUS LIGHTNING REVEALING A TROOP OF **FORTY STYGIANS**, BOUND SOUTHWARD TOWARD THE FORESTS BEYOND KUSH.

KEEP UP WITH ME, CURSE YOUR DUSKY SOULS!

STORMS OR NO, WE MUST SOON REACH THE **BLACK VILLAGES** -- ONES WE CAN TAKE BY SURPRISE!

KING CTESPHON, BLAST HER SOUL, WANTS **SLAVES** --

AND, IF WE DO NOT FIND SOME ERE LONG, WE **OURSELVES** SHALL --

WHAT THE **DEVIL**?

BEHOLD, BROTHERS -- **SHELTER**, BY ALL THE SERPENTS OF FATHER SET!

WE ARE IN **LUCK**!

MY CAPTAIN -- THIS PLACE SEEMS NOT **SAFE**, SOMEHOW! SEE HOW IT'S CRUMBLING --!

THEN SLEEP OUT IN THE **RAIN**, IF YOU PREFER, DOG!

NO? I DID NOT THINK SO. THEN **COME**...!

OUTSIDE, THE **STORM** BELLOWS AND FLASHES... AND STREAMS OF WATER POUR LIKE LITTLE WATERFALLS THROUGH GAPS IN THE MASONRY...

BUT SOON, WITHIN THE BLACK CITADEL, THE STYGIANS ARE WARM BEFORE THEIR **FIRE**... WARM AND **SAFE**, OR SO THEY IMAGINE.

WAKENED BY THE SECOND CLOUDBURST, HOWEVER, CONAN-- WATCHING FROM OVERHEAD-- KNOWS BETTER.

HE MIGHT BE TEMPTED TO GO DOWN AND TRY TO **JOIN** THEM, TRUSTING THAT SUCH A TROOP-- EVEN OF XENOPHOBIC STYGIANS-- CAN ALWAYS USE ANOTHER GOOD SWORD--

--BUT THAT HE **CANNOT LEAVE THE BALCONY!**

FOR, THOUGH HE DOES NOT SEE THE SHADOWY **CONCLAVE OF GHOSTS** HE BEHELD IN HIS DREAM, HE SEES--**SOMETHING**-- LOOMING DARK AND AMORPHOUS AT THE FAR END OF THE BALCONY...

AND, SOMEHOW, HE KNOWS THAT IF HE ENTERS IT TO REACH THE STAIRS-- HE'LL NOT COME **OUT** AGAIN ALIVE!

YET, IF THE STYGIANS HAVE DISTRACTED CONAN, THEY HAVE DONE NO LESS TO THAT **PHANTOM SHAPE** ITSELF.

FOR, HERE IS **LIVING FLESH-- VITAL FORCE** ENOUGH TO GLUT THE PHANTASMAL LUSTS OF THE GHOSTS **THRICE OVER**...

AND SO-- SLOWLY, UNSEEN, ONE MORE SHADOW AMONG MANY, THOUGH OF A FAR DEEPER BLACKNESS-- IT BEGINS TO DRIFT DOWN THE STAIRWAY TOWARD THE GREAT HALL BELOW.

THEN, AS MORE AND MORE STYGIANS BEGIN TO *DOZE OFF*, MANY SOTTED WITH BAD WINE...

KASPA! YOUR WATCH, DOG!

EH? LET *MERAP* TAKE IT, CAPTAIN! I'M--

THE MAN IS NOT DRUNK ENOUGH TO GO ON, UNDER HIS LEADER'S WITHERING GLARE...

...THOUGH IT TAKES SCANT KNOWLEDGE OF STYGIAN TO UNDERSTAND THE *OBSCENITIES* WHICH HE MUTTERS UNDER HIS BREATH AS, DONNING HELMET AND ARMOR, HE MOVES TOWARD THE OUTER DOORWAY.

FOR A FLEETING INSTANT, CONAN IS TEMPTED TO *CALL OUT* TO THE STYGIANS-- TO WARN THEM OF THEIR DANGER, OF--

OF WHAT? OF *SHADOWS?* OF *DREAMS?* HE'D SOUND LIKE A *MADMAN,* HE KNOWS...

AND STYGIANS ARE NOTORIOUSLY *UNFRIENDLY* TO FOREIGN-BORN UNFORTUNATES.

THEN, WHEN THE SENTRY HAS GONE AND EVEN THE DOUR CAPTAIN HAS FALLEN ASLEEP-- A *GRIM SHAPE* BEGINS TO FORM AMONG AND ABOVE THE SNORING BAND OF SLAVERS--

-- GROWING SLOWLY, OH SO SLOWLY, OUT OF WAVERING CLOUDS OF INSUBSTANTIAL *SHADOWS.*

CONAN FEELS HIS NAPE-HAIRS RISE AND HIS SKIN CRAWL WITH *REVULSION* AS HE STARES DOWN AT THE UNBELIEVABLE SCENE...

THE **LEADER** OF THE SLAVERS IS THE FIRST TO WAKE, WIDE-EYED...

...AND THUS, THE FIRST TO **DIE!**

YAAAAAA

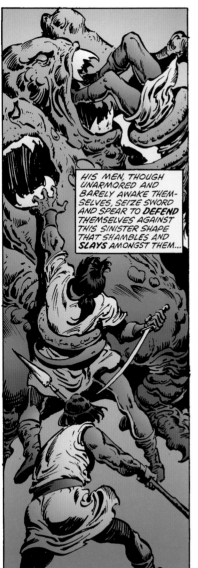

HIS MEN, THOUGH UNARMORED AND BARELY AWAKE THEMSELVES, SEIZE SWORD AND SPEAR TO **DEFEND** THEMSELVES AGAINST THIS SINISTER SHAPE THAT SHAMBLES AND **SLAYS** AMONGST THEM...

BUT, WHETHER IT IS A **HEAD** OR AN **ARM** OF THE THING THAT IS SEVERED BY A STYGIAN BLADE--

--THE REACTION IS STILL THE SAME--

A **NEW** MEMBER, SPROUTING ON THE INSTANT FROM THE BULBOUS, MISSHAPEN BODY--

--READY TO DEAL **DEATH** ONCE MORE!

BY NOW, THOSE STYGIANS THAT STILL LIVE ARE ALL ON THEIR FEET--

--BUT THE MONSTER IS IN THEIR VERY *MIDST*, TEARING AND RENDING, EVEN AS THEY SCRAMBLE CONFUSEDLY FOR THEIR WEAPONS... OR FOR THE DOOR.

WHEN HE HAS SEEN AT LEAST A *DOZEN* OF THE DUSKY SLAVERS TAKE THE PLUNGE INTO DARKSOME DEATH--

--CONAN DECIDES IT IS TIME FOR HIM TO *DEPART*.

NO USE THROWING *GOOD* BLOOD AFTER *BAD*.

HE DOES *NOT* LEAVE, HOWEVER, BY WAY OF THE GREAT HALL--

--NOT WHEN THERE'S A MORE *DIRECT* EXIT, JUST PAST WHERE THE LOATHSOME SHADOW-THING HAD FORMERLY WRITHED AND MURMURED IN ITS HUNDRED-HEADED WAY.

THE RAIN HAS SLACKENED TO A *DRIZZLE* NOW, THOUGH THE OUTER STONES STILL ARE WET, SLIPPERY...

...AND A *BREAKING VINE* WOULD SEND EVEN A SURE-FOOTED CIMMERIAN TO AN UNTIMELY END.

THE **SCREAMS OF THE DYING** STILL SOUND IN HIS EARS AS HE DROPS LIGHTLY TO THE COURTYARD--

--AND HEADS FOR THE GREAT BLACK **MARE** WHICH BELONGS TO THE SLAVER-CAPTAIN.

CORRECTION-- **BELONGED.**

THEN, JUST AS HE NEARS THE FRIGHTENED, EARTH-PAWING STEEDS--

HEEEYAAAH!

WH--? THE **SENTRY!**

YOU **SURVIVED** THE SLAUGHTER WITHIN, STYGIAN, ONLY BECAUSE YOU'D DONNED YOUR ARMOR FOR THE WATCH.

JOIN ME ON A PAIR OF **FAST HORSES,** AND WE'LL BOTH--

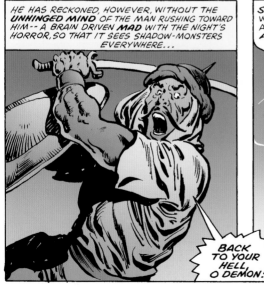

HE HAS RECKONED, HOWEVER, WITHOUT THE **UNHINGED MIND** OF THE MAN RUSHING TOWARD HIM-- A BRAIN DRIVEN **MAD** WITH THE NIGHT'S HORROR, SO THAT IT SEES SHADOW-MONSTERS EVERYWHERE...

BACK TO YOUR **HELL,** O DEMON!

STOP, FOOL! WE CAN FORM A **ROGUES' ALLIANCE** TILL--

YOU **SLEW** THEM-- BUT YOU WON'T GET **ME,** DEVIL-THING! I'LL--

YOU'LL *DIE*, I FEAR--MAD *OR* SANE!

GRRRRK

YOU DON'T LEAVE A MAN MUCH *CHOICE*.

EH? NO MORE *CRIES* FROM WITHIN?

I'LL WAGER IT'S *NOT* BECAUSE SOMEONE FOUND THE HEART OF A CREATURE THAT *HAS* NO HEART.

I DOUBT IF THE THING CAN *LEAVE* ITS CITADEL--

--BUT, I'LL *NOT* WAIT TO FIND OUT!

HURRY, HORSE!

THE KING-DOM OF *KUSH*, SOME DAYS NORTH, IS MORE OR LESS *CIVILIZED*, THEY SAY--

--BUT EVEN *THAT* WILL BE A RELIEF, AFTER THIS NIGHT'S HORROR!

WITH EVERY STRIDE OF THOSE FLYING HOOVES, THE CASTLE OF ANCIENT EVIL FALLS FURTHER BEHIND.

SOMEWHERE BEYOND THE CIRCLE OF DEAD GRASS, PERHAPS THE *HUNGRY LIONS* STILL PROWL...BUT CONAN CARES LITTLE.

AFTER THE GHOSTLY TERRORS OF THE BLACK CITADEL, HE WILL GLADLY TAKE HIS *CHANCES* WITH MERE CARNIVORES...

...BEASTS THAT DEVOUR YOUR BODY ONLY, NOT YOUR *SOUL*...!

NEXT ISSUE: **THE SNOUT IN THE DARK!**

"Know, O prince, that between the years when the oceans drank Atlantis and the gleaming cities, and the rise of the sons of Aryas, there was an Age undreamed of, when shining kingdoms lay spread across the world like blue mantles beneath the stars.
"Hither came Conan, the Cimmerian, black-haired, sullen-eyed, sword in hand, a thief, a reaver, a slayer, with gigantic melancholies and gigantic mirth, to tread the jeweled thrones of the Earth under his sandaled feet."
—*The Nemedian Chronicles.*

STAN LEE PRESENTS: CONAN THE BARBARIAN®

CHAOS IN THE LAND CALLED KUSH!

CONTINUING HIS NORTHWARD TREK BACK TOWARD THE HYBORIAN LANDS-- BUT HELPED NOW BY POSSESSION OF A STYGIAN HORSE AND STYGIAN LIGHT ARMOR-- CONAN AT LAST REACHES *KUSH.*

YET, IF HE KNEW WHAT AWAITS HIM IN *MEROË,* CAPITAL OF THAT SEMI-CIVILIZED BLACK KINGDOM... PERHAPS HE WOULD GIVE IT A WIDE AND WARY BERTH...!

ROY THOMAS
WRITER / EDITOR

JOHN BUSCEMA & ERNIE CHAN
ILLUSTRATORS

JOE ROSEN, LETTERER

JIM SHOOTER
CONSULTING EDITOR

ADAPTED FROM THE STORY "THE SNOUT IN THE DARK" BY *L. SPRAGUE DE CAMP & LIN CARTER*
FEATURING THE EPIC HERO CREATED BY *ROBERT E. HOWARD*

FOR, SOMEWHERE IN THAT CITY, AT THIS VERY MOMENT, A MAN *AWAKENS* SLOWLY... HIS SENSES STILL SLUGGISH FROM THE *FEAST* THE NIGHT BEFORE...

UHHH-- TOO MUCH *WINE!* WHERE AM--?

THEN, THE *CHAIN* CLANKING ON HIS WRIST REMINDS HIM:

HE, *AMBOOLA OF KUSH,* IS FETTERED IN A *CELL*-- IN THE PRISON INTO WHICH *QUEEN TANANDA* HAD HIM THROWN!

THE WINE...WAS *DRUGGED,* THEN! BUT WHY--?

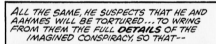

HEAD THROBBING, HE FORCES HIMSELF TO THINK BACK...

ALL THE SAME, HE SUSPECTS THAT HE AND AAHMES WILL BE TORTURED...TO WRING FROM THEM THE FULL *DETAILS* OF THE IMAGINED CONSPIRACY, SO THAT--

WHO'S THERE?

SUDDENLY, AMBOOLA SENSES A LIVING BREATHING *PRESENCE* IN THE CELL THERE WITH HIM...

...TO REMEMBER HOW TWO VIRTUAL *GIANTS* OF THE QUEEN'S GUARD LAID HANDS UPON HIM... AND UPON ONE OTHER--

SO, YOU AND MY COUSIN, THE *LORD AAHMES,* WOULD PLOT TO *OVER-THROW* ME, WOULD YOU?

WELL, YOU SHALL SEE THE FATE THAT BEFALLS *TRAITORS AGAINST QUEEN TANANDA!*

BUT, MY QUEEN-- I SWEAR THAT WE *NEVER*--

THEN, HE WAS HUSTLED AWAY TO A DIFFERENT CELL FROM POOR, EASY-GOING *AAHMES*...WHO WAS DOUBTLESS AS *INNOCENT* OF THE CHARGES AS AMBOOLA KNOWS HE HIMSELF TO BE.

YET, TURNING, HE BE-HOLDS ONLY A SHAPE-LESS GRAY *FOG* WHICH SWIRLS IN THE GLOOM LIKE A NEST OF COILING SERPENTS...

WHAT IN *AJUJO'S* NAME--?

MERE CLOUDS OF DISTURBED *DUST*-- SOME NIGHTTIME *MIST*-- OR--?

THEN, AN *ICY HAND* CLUTCHES THE KUSHITE'S HEART, WHICH HAS NEVER BEFORE THIS HOUR KNOWN *FEAR*...

...AS THE SEETHING MISTS BEGIN TO CONGEAL INTO A *SOLID AND TERRIBLE FORM!*

K-KEEP BACK!

WITHIN SECONDS, THE HULKING FORM IS *COMPLETE*-- A THING HUGE AND MISSHAPEN AMID THE GATHERED SHADOWS--

GRONK

-- A MONSTER WHICH, THOUGH BESTIAL IN FORM, WALKS ON *TWO THICK LEGS*--

--AND NOW *HURLS* ITSELF TOWARD THE HELPLESS AMBOOLA!

N-NO!

AWNK AWNK

N NOOOOO

IN A FEW MOMENTS, IT IS OVER...

...AND THE GRAYISH, SHAMBLING THING IS *GONE* FROM THE CELL...

...DISSOLVED BACK INTO THE IMPLACABLE *MIST* FROM WHICH IT HAD TAKEN GRISLY FORM.

TUTHMES! LORD TUTHMES!

LET ME IN! THE DEVIL IS LOOSE AGAIN IN MEROË!

WHY DO YOU DISTURB ME AT THIS HOUR, AFARI?

IT IS AMBOOLA! HE IS DEAD-- IN THE RED TOWER!

WHAT? QUEEN TANANDA DARED TO EXECUTE THE COMMANDER OF THE BLACK SPEARS?

NO, NO-- SHE'D NOT BE SUCH A FOOL, SURELY...

SOMETHING GOT INTO HIS CELL-- THE DEMON OF WHOM THE PEOPLE MUTTER-- THE THING THEY CALL THE INVISIBLE TERROR!

CALM YOUR-SELF, MAN! WHEN WAS THIS DONE?

SOME TIME ABOUT MIDNIGHT, THE GUARDS HEARD HIM CRY OUT.

THEY FOUND HIM SLAIN-- HIS THROAT TORN, HIS SKULL SMASHED-- AS IF BY SOME WILD ANIMAL!

I WAS SLEEPING NEARBY, AS YOU BADE ME.

BIDDING THE GUARDS TO SAY NOTHING TO ANYONE, I CAME STRAIGHT HERE.

IT WAS THE DEMON, I TELL YOU--!

TSK, TSK, AFARI...YOU KNOW QUEEN TANANDA'S MAD RAGES-- SHE MIGHT WELL HAVE HAD AMBOOLA SLAIN AND THE CORPSE MISTREATED THUS, MIGHT SHE NOT?

I-- SEE WHAT YOU MEAN, TUTHMES...

GOOD, THEN GO NOW-- AND STRIKE BEFORE THE QUEEN CAN LEARN OF THE DEED!

FIRST, TAKE SOME BLACK SPEARMEN TO THE RED TOWER-- AND SLAY THE GUARDS, FOR SLEEPING AT THEIR DUTY!

BE SURE YOU LET IT BE KNOWN YOU DO IT BY MY ORDERS.

THAT WILL SHOW THE BLACKS OF THE CITY THAT I HAVE AVENGED THEIR COMMANDER-- AND REMOVE A WEAPON FROM TANANDA'S HAND.

THE GUARDS MUST BE KILLED BEFORE SHE CAN HAVE IT DONE!

THEN, WHEN YOU'VE SPREAD THE WORDS TO THE OTHER CHIEF *NOBLES*, GO INTO THE OUTER CITY AND FIND OLD *AGEERA, THE WITCH-SMELLER!*

BUT, HOW CAN ONE *LIE* TO THAT DEVIL, WHO CAN MAKE CORPSES RISE AND TALK?

DON'T LIE TO HIM-- SIMPLY HINT TO HIM OF YOUR OWN, ER, *SUSPICIONS*. NOW HURRY!

AS SOON AS AFARI HAS DEPARTED INTO THE WANING NIGHT...

MURU!

I AM HERE, MASTER.

IS *IT* BACK IN ITS CELL?

IT IS.

I ONLY WISH I COULD BE SURE IT WILL ALWAYS *OBEY* YOUR COMMANDS, MURU... RATHER THAN *SLAY* YOU AND FLEE BACK TO WHATEVER UNHOLY DIMENSIONS IT CALLS HOME.

THE *SPELL* I LEARNED FROM MY FORMER MASTER, THE EXILED STYGIAN WIZARD, HAS NEVER YET FAILED ME.

YOU WIZARDS SPEND *MOST* OF YOUR TIME IN EXILE, IT SEEMS...

STILL, HOW DO I KNOW THAT SOMEDAY AN ENEMY WILL NOT *BRIBE* YOU TO TURN THE MONSTER LOOSE ON *ME?*

OH, MASTER, THINK *NOT* SUCH THOUGHTS! WITHOUT YOUR PROTECTION, WHERE WOULD I *GO?*

THE *KUSHITES* DESPISE ME, FOR I AM NOT OF THEIR RACE...

AND, FOR REASONS YOU KNOW WELL, I CANNOT RETURN SOUTH TO MY NATIVE *KORDAFA*.

TRUE ENOUGH...

WELL, TAKE GOOD CARE OF YOUR PIG-NOSED DEMON, MURU... FOR WE MAY HAVE *MORE* USE OF IT SOON.

THAT LOOSE-TONGUED FOOL *AFARI* WILL SOON SPREAD THE TALE OF AMBOOLA'S *MURDER*...

THE BREACH 'TWIXT QUEEN TANANDA AND HER LORDS WILL WIDEN, AND *I* SHALL REAP THE BENEFIT.

OF COURSE, AFARI DOESN'T REALIZE THAT I KNOW *HE* BEGAN THE WHOLE CHARADE-- WITH HIS *FALSE ACCUSATIONS* AGAINST AMBOOLA AND AAHMES, ALL ON HIS OWN.

HIS ULTIMATE AMBITION IS TO *WED* TANANDA, AND RULE KUSH AS ROYAL CONSORT.

WHEN *I* AM KING, I SHALL NEED A MORE *TRUSTWORTHY* TOOL THAN AFARI.

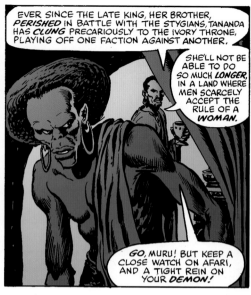

EVER SINCE THE LATE KING, HER BROTHER, *PERISHED* IN BATTLE WITH THE STYGIANS, TANANDA HAS *CLUNG* PRECARIOUSLY TO THE IVORY THRONE, PLAYING OFF ONE FACTION AGAINST ANOTHER.

SHE'LL NOT BE ABLE TO DO SO MUCH *LONGER*, IN A LAND WHERE MEN SCARCELY ACCEPT THE RULE OF A *WOMAN*.

GO, MURU! BUT KEEP A CLOSE WATCH ON AFARI, AND A TIGHT REIN ON YOUR *DEMON!*

AS I SAID... WE SHALL NEED THE CREATURE *AGAIN*...!

ALONE NOW, TUTHMES STRIDES TO THE SPACIOUS BALCONY OF HIS PALACE...

...FROM WHICH HE CAN SEE THE SILENT STREETS OF THE *INNER CITY*, WITH ITS OWN PALACES, ITS GARDENS...

...AND THAT GREAT INNER *SQUARE* INTO WHICH, AT AN INSTANT'S NOTICE, A THOUSAND *BLACK HORSEMEN* CAN RIDE FROM THE ADJOINING BARRACKS TO PROTECT HIS OWN RACE'S RULE.

BEYOND THE INNER CITY'S GREAT BRONZE GATES, HE BEHOLDS THE *OUTER CITY*...

...WHOSE BLACKS ARE DESCENDED FROM THE *ORIGINAL* INHABITANTS OF MEROË, RATHER THAN FROM THEIR LONG-AGO STYGIAN CONQUERORS.

NONE BUT THE *RULING CASTE* LIVE IN THE *INNER CITY*...

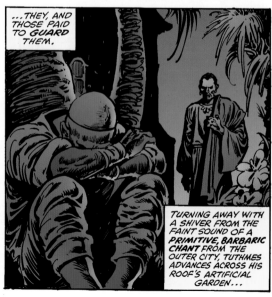

...THEY, AND THOSE PAID TO *GUARD* THEM.

TURNING AWAY WITH A SHIVER FROM THE FAINT SOUND OF A *PRIMITIVE, BARBARIC CHANT* FROM THE OUTER CITY, TUTHMES ADVANCES ACROSS HIS ROOF'S ARTIFICIAL GARDEN...

...TO STIR TO WAKEFULNESS A FIGURE SLEEPING THERE:

THERE IS NO NEED FOR SPEECH, SHUBBA.

THE DEED IS DONE-- AMBOOLA IS DEAD...

AND, BY DAWN, ALL MEROË WILL KNOW HE WAS MURDERED BY TANANDA.

AND THE-- THE DEVIL--?

SAFELY BACK IN ITS CELL.

NOW, SHUBBA-- SEARCH AMONG THE SHEMITES TILL YOU FIND A SUITABLE WOMAN, AND BRING HER SPEEDILY HERE.

RETURN WITHIN THE MOON, AND I WILL GIVE YOU HER WEIGHT IN SILVER.

FAIL ME... AND I WILL HANG YOUR HEAD FROM YONDER PALM TREE.

I... WILL NOT FAIL, O TUTHMES.

JUST THEN, FROM THE OUTER CITY, THE DUSKY MAN HEARS AN OMINOUS DRUM BEGIN... A SUDDEN CLAMOR OF FURIOUS SHOUTS WELLING UP TO THE STARS...

THEY HAVE HEARD THAT AMBOOLA IS DEAD.

AND AGAIN, A STRONG SHUDDER SHAKES HIS FRAME.

DAWN IN THE OUTER CITY--

IN THE MARKET SQUARE, THE HOT SUN SOON BLAZES DOWN ON ALL...

...THE SWEAT, MIRTH, ANGER, STRENGTH, SQUALOR, AND VIGOR OF THE BLACK PEOPLE OF KUSH.

THEN, SUDDENLY, THERE COMES A NEW NOTE IN THE TIMBRE... AS WITH A CLATTER OF HOOVES, HALF A DOZEN *HORSEMEN* RIDE BY IN THE DIRECTION OF THE GREAT GATE OF THE *INNER CITY*...

...SIX HORSEMEN... AND ONE DUSKY BROWN *WOMAN*:

QUEEN TANANDA...!

BLACK FACES GROW SULLEN AS SHE RIDES BY...AND HOARSE WHISPERS GROW TO AN AUDIBLE, SINISTER MURMUR...

WHY DOES *SHE* RIDE OUT AMONG US?

AYE. ISN'T SHE HAPPY ENOUGH LORDING IT OVER THE *INNER CITY* WHILE WE BOW AND SCRAPE OUTSIDE?

THE PEOPLE GROW *UGLY*, HIGHNESS. I TOLD YOU IT WAS *FOLLY* TO RIDE TO THE HUNT THROUGH THE OUTER CITY TODAY.

ALL THE BLACK DOGS IN KUSH SHALL NOT KEEP ME FROM MY *HUNTING.*

IF ANY THREATEN, *RIDE THEM DOWN!*

EASIER SAID THAN *DONE*, HIGHNESS.

THEY ARE COMING EVEN FROM THEIR HOUSES, AND MASSING THICK ALONG THE STREET-- *LOOK THERE!*

WE PASS BY THEIR *DEVIL-DEVIL HOUSE,* WHERE THEY WORSHIP THEIR ANCESTRAL GOD *JULLAH!*

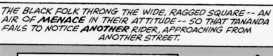

THE BLACK FOLK THRONG THE WIDE, RAGGED SQUARE -- AN AIR OF *MENACE* IN THEIR ATTITUDE -- SO THAT TANANDA FAILS TO NOTICE *ANOTHER* RIDER, APPROACHING FROM ANOTHER STREET.

SINCE HE IS WHITE RATHER THAN BLACK OR BROWN, HE WOULD ORDINARILY HAVE ATTRACTED ATTENTION...BUT NOT *THIS* MORNING OF MORNINGS...

...AS ABRUPTLY, FROM WHAT THE RULING CASTE CONTEMPTUOUSLY CALL THE "DEVIL-DEVIL HOUSE"--

AIEEE! IT IS OLD *AGEERA,* THE WITCH-SMELLER!

THERE SHE RIDES -- SHE WHOSE HANDS ARE DIPPED IN *BLOOD* --

-- SHE WHO MURDERED AMBOOLA!

HIS SHOUT IS THE SPARK THAT SETS OFF THE EXPLOSION, AS--

DEATH TO TANANDA!

AAAGK

AN INSTANT MORE, AND A *HUN-DRED BLACK HANDS* ARE CLAW-ING AT THE LEGS OF THE RIDERS--

--TEARING THEM FROM THEIR STEEDS--BEATING AND *STAMPING* THEM TO DEATH!

TANANDA, BESET AT LAST BY TERROR, *SCREAMS* AS HER HORSE REARS--

--SCREAMS EVEN LOUDER WHEN SHE SEES THAT SHE HAS FALLEN INTO THE HANDS OF THE *ANGRY MOB!*

RELEASE ME, YOU FILTHY RABBLE! I'LL--

BUT, HER WORDS FALL ON EARS DEAFENED BY THE PAIN *SHE'S* DEALT OUT, IN TIMES PAST--

--AND SHE SEES, WITH SHUDDER-ING HORROR, A *STONE* CLUTCHED IN A HAND WHICH COMES CLOSER-- *CLOSER--!*

N-NOOOO

THEN, THE WHOLE CROWD SEEMS TO STAGGER BEFORE A *HORSE-MAN* ON A POWERFUL STEED--

YYYY

--AND MEN FALL *SHRIEKING* UNDER DARK, FLAILING HOOVES!

YET, FROM SOMEWHERE IN THE PRESS, A *SPEAR* IS HURLED--

WNEEEE

--AND THE VALIANT STALLION GOES DOWN!

THE *RIDER*, HOWEVER, LANDS ON HIS FEET, ALREADY SMITING RIGHT AND LEFT...

...UNTIL, STILL FIGHTING FIERCELY AND WORDLESSLY, HE REACHES THE TERRIFIED *TANANDA*.

GRRGG

COVERING HER WITH HIS SHIELD, HE FALLS BACK, CUTTING A RUTHLESS PATH...

...THEN STANDING *BEFORE* HER, BEATING BACK THE FROTHING, SCREAMING ONSLAUGHT!

AAAA AAA

THEN, WITH A CLATTER OF HOOVES--

THE PALACE GUARDS!

LIKE A DUSKY WAVE, THE COMPANY OF GUARDSMEN SWEEP INTO THE SQUARE, DRIVING THE RIOTERS BEFORE THEM.

HO, TO QUEEN TANANDA!

YELLING IN SUDDEN PANIC, THE KUSHITES FLEE INTO THE SIDE-STREETS, LEAVING A SCORE OF THEIR BODIES LITTERING THE AREA.

THE CAPTAIN OF THE GUARD -- A GIANT BLACK RE-SPLENDENT IN HIS CRIMSON SILK AND GOLD-WORKED HARNESS APPROACHES AND DISMOUNTS...

YOU WERE *LONG* IN COMING.

I *SWEAR* TO YOU, MY QUEEN -- WE --

EVEN AS HE STAMMERS, TANANDA MAKES A SIGN TO THE MEN *BEHIND* HIM...

...AND ONE OF THEM DISPOSES OF THE MAN WHO, MERE MINUTES BEFORE, LED THEM FORTH INTO BATTLE.

AIEEE

THOUGH BLEEDING FROM A SCORE OF SCRATCHES, TANANDA NOW FACES HER *RESCUER*, WHO CANNOT HELP BETRAYING A FRANK ADMIRATION FOR HER COOL BEARING... AMONG OTHER THINGS.

WHO ARE YOU?

I AM *CONAN*, A CIMMERIAN.

CIMMERIAN? I HAVE NEVER HEARD OF SUCH A PLACE.

YOU WEAR A STYGIAN HELMET AND SHIELD. ARE YOU A *STYGIAN* OF SOME SORT I'VE NOT SEEN BEFORE?

I GOT THE ARMOR FROM A STYGIAN... BUT I HAD TO *KILL* THE FOOL FIRST.

WHAT DO YOU, THEN, IN *MEROË*, CAPITAL OF KUSH?

I'M A *WANDERER*, WITH A SWORD FOR HIRE-- I CAME HERE TO SEEK MY FORTUNE.

HE THINKS IT BEST TO OMIT REFERENCE TO HIS PAST CAREERS AS A PIRATE AND AS WAR-CHIEF OF THE SAVAGE *BAMULA* TRIBE TO THE SOUTH.

I WILL HIRE YOUR SWORD, I THINK. WHAT IS YOUR PRICE?

WHAT PRICE DO YOU OFFER?

I'M A PENNILESS FREEBOOTER... AND NOW, ALAS, *AFOOT* AS WELL.

NO, BY SET! YOU ARE PENNILESS NO LONGER, BUT *CAPTAIN OF MY ROYAL GUARD!*

WILL A HUNDRED PIECES OF *GOLD* A MONTH BUY YOUR LOYALTY?

CONAN GLANCES CASUALLY AT THE SPRAWLING FIGURE OF THE *PREVIOUS* CAPTAIN, WHO LIES IN SILK, STEEL, AND BLOOD.

STILL, THE SIGHT DOES NOT DIM THE ZEST OF HIS SUDDEN GRIN.

I THINK SO, YES...!

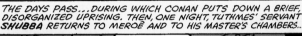

THE DAYS PASS...DURING WHICH CONAN PUTS DOWN A BRIEF, DISORGANIZED UPRISING. THEN, ONE NIGHT, TUTHMES' SERVANT *SHUBBA* RETURNS TO MEROË AND TO HIS MASTER'S CHAMBERS...

I HAVE FOUND A *WOMAN* SUCH AS YOU DESIRED, SIRE...

...A *NEMEDIAN*, CAPTURED FROM A TRADING VESSEL OUT OF ARGOS.

LET ME SEE HER.

I PAID THE SHEMITE SLAVE-TRADERS MANY GOLD-PIECES FOR--

COME HERE, WENCH!

YES-- *PLEASE!* D-DON'T STRIKE ME AGAIN--!

SHE'S A FINE BIT OF MERCHANDISE-- IF I WERE NOT GAMBLING FOR A *THRONE*, I MIGHT BE TEMPTED TO KEEP HER FOR MYSELF.

HAVE YOU TAUGHT HER *KUSHITE*, AS I COMMANDED?

AYE, SIRE... ALONG THE CARAVAN TRAIL. HER NAME IS *DIANA.*

LISTEN TO ME, GIRL...

I AM GOING TO GIVE YOU TO THE *QUEEN OF KUSH* AS A PRESENT...A SLAVE.

BUT, YOU WILL RECEIVE ORDERS REGULARLY FROM *ME*...AND YOU SHALL NOT FAIL TO CARRY THEM OUT!

BUT, I-- I DON'T KNOW WHAT TO--

SILENCE! JUST LISTEN! THE QUEEN IS *CRUEL*, SO BEWARE OF ROILING HER.

BUT YOU SHALL SAY *NOTHING*, EVEN IF TORTURED, OF YOUR CONTINUING CONNEC-TION WITH *ME.*

AND, LEST YOU FANCY YOURSELF OUT OF MY *REACH* IN THE ROYAL PALACE AND BE TEMPTED TO *DISOBEY*--

--I SHALL DEMONSTRATE MY *POWER* TO YOU.

COME!

DOWN A FLIGHT OF STONE STAIRS HE LEADS HER, AND INTO A LONG AND DIMLY LIT ROOM...

...A CHAMBER DIVIDED IN HALF BY A *WALL OF CRYSTAL.*

THAT WALL IS A YARD THICK-- AND STRONG ENOUGH TO RESIST THE LUNGE OF A *BULL ELEPHANT.*

NOW *WATCH!*

ABRUPTLY, THE LIGHT GOES OUT-- AND THEN, *LIGHT* BEGINS TO GLOW OUT OF THE BLACKNESS...

SOMETHING BEGINS TO *FORM* THERE-- SOMETHING WHICH MAKES HER TREMBLE WITH UNREASONING *PANIC*--

SHE SEES A MALFORMED, HIDEOUS HEAD-- A BESTIAL *SNOUT*--CHISEL-LIKE *TEETH*-- AND *BRISTLES!*

AND THEN-- THE HORROR MOVES *TOWARD* HER!

NO! NNOOO!

GRONNK

LITTLE FOOL! EVEN *HE,* WHO IS MY SERVANT AS FULLY AS YOU ARE, CANNOT GET TO YOU THROUGH THAT WALL OF UNBREAKABLE CRYSTAL.

BUT, DO NOT FAIL ME-- FOR, IF YOU DO, HE WILL *SEARCH YOU OUT* WHEREVER YOU MAY BE--

--AND HE WILL--

WHEN TUTHMES WHISPERS SOMETHING ELSE INTO DIANA'S EAR... SHE *FAINTS.*

A BLACK WOMAN AWAITS UPSTAIRS WITH ORDERS TO REVIVE HER, TO SEE THAT SHE HAS FOOD AND WINE, AND TO BATHE, PERFUME, AND CLOTHE HER.

AFTER ALL, TOMORROW DIANA OF NEMEDIA BECOMES THE *SLAVE OF QUEEN TANANDA.*

AND INDEED, THE NEXT MORNING...

COME, NORTHBORN WENCH! WHY SUCH A *HANGDOG* LOOK?

YOU'RE TO BE HANDMAIDEN TO A *QUEEN*...FOR AS LONG AS YOU *LIVE!*

OVERHEAD, THE SKY HAS A STEELY LOOK, AS CLOUDS PILE UP IN THE WEST -- THE *END* OF KUSH'S DRY SEASON IS AT HAND.

IN THE MONTHS SINCE THE SLAVERS CAPTURED HER, LIFE HAS BEEN A *NIGHTMARE* FOR DIANA.

SHE HAS COMFORTED HERSELF WITH THE THOUGHT THAT NOTHING LASTS FOREVER... AND THAT THINGS WERE SO BAD, THEY WERE BOUND TO IMPROVE.

INSTEAD, THEY HAVE ONLY *WORSENED*...AND SHE FEARS FOR HER LIFE, IN MORE WAYS THAN ONE.

FALAHA, I BRING HER MAJESTY A *GIFT*... FROM MY LORD *TUTHMES.*

CURRYING FAVOR AGAIN, IS HE?

WELL... THIS WAY, GIRL.

...AND DO NOT FORGET TO *BOW LOW* BEFORE THE QUEEN WHEN I PRESENT YOU TO HER!

IF YOU ARE INSOLENT, SHE MAY WELL TAKE IT OUT ON *ME*... AND I, IN TURN, ON *YOU.*

MOMENTS LATER, IN A LARGE CHAMBER FITTED OUT WITH ORNATE OPULENCE FIT EVEN FOR A STYGIAN PRINCESS...

A GIFT FROM LORD *TUTHMES*, MY QUEEN.

SHE IS *NEMEDIAN*, BUT SPEAKS A BIT OF *KUSHITE.* SHE--

LEAVE US.

Y-YES, MY QUEEN.

THEN, AS SOON THE MAJOR DOMO OF THE PALACE HAS DEPARTED...

SPEAK, WENCH! *WHY* DID TUTHMES SEND YOU TO THE PALACE?

YOU'LL *ANSWER* ME, IF YOU KNOW WHAT'S GOOD FOR YOU.

I-- I DO NOT KNOW-- WHERE *AM* I? WH-WHO ARE *YOU*?

I AM *QUEEN TANANDA* OF MEROË, FOOL-- NOW ANSWER ME!

I KNOW *NOT* THE ANSWER, MY LADY. ALL I KNOW IS THAT LORD TUTHMES SENT ME...AS A *GIFT*. HE--

YOU LIE!

TUTHMES IS EATEN UP WITH *AMBITION,* AND WOULD NOT MAKE ME A GIFT WITHOUT AN ULTERIOR REASON.

GUARD! YOU KNOW WHAT TO DO!

IT IS *DONE,* MY QUEEN.

P-PLEASE! I KNOW NOTHING!

I KNOW NOTHING!

YOU MAY KNOW *LITTLE*, MY DEAR-- BUT IT IS CERTAINLY FAR MORE THAN *NOTHING*.

AND, WHATEVER YOU DO KNOW ABOUT TUTHMES' LITTLE SCHEMES, YOU SHALL *TELL* ME BEFORE A FEW MINUTES MORE HAVE PASSED.

NOW, ONCE MORE-- *WILL YOU SPEAK*?

EVERY FIBRE WITHIN HER URGES DIANA TO TELL THE VILE QUEEN WHAT PRECIOUS LITTLE SHE KNOWS--

BUT THEN, SHE REMEMBERS THE *SNOUT IN THE DARK*-- AND REMAINS FEARFULLY SILENT.

YOU ARE *BRAVE*-- OR ELSE AFRAID OF SOMETHING BESIDES MY *WHIP*.

WELL, WE SHALL SEE HOW LONG *THAT* LASTS, SHALL WE NOT?

WE SHALL *NOT*!

NOW *THAT*, DEAR QUEEN, I'D LOVE TO SEE YOU *TRY*.

AND, IF YOU DON'T LET THAT GIRL DOWN FROM THERE-- *THAT'S EXACTLY WHAT YOU'LL HAVE TO DO*!

WHAT? YOU *DARE* INTRUDE UPON ME *HERE*, CONAN OF CIMMERIA?

BEGONE-- OR YOU'LL TASTE THE LASH BEFORE EVEN *SHE* DOES!

NEXT. ISSUE: THE **DAY** OF THE **DEMON!**

THAT WAS ONLY MY *SECONDARY* REASON FOR COMING, TANANDA-- I AM ALSO HERE AS *CAPTAIN* OF YOUR ROYAL GUARD.

WHAT'S THIS *FOLLY* I JUST HEARD OF, FROM YOUR MINISTER *AFAR!*?

HE SAID YOU PLAN TO LET THE *BLACKS* INTO THE INNER CITY TO WATCH THE EXECUTION OF *LORD AAHMES.*

HAVE YOU TAKEN LEAVE OF YOUR *SENSES,* WOMAN?

CAREFUL, CONAN! YOU SKIRT THE EDGES OF MY *ANGER.*

FORCING THE LOWER CLASSES TO WATCH AAHMES BURN FOR HIS *TREASON* WILL SHOW THE DOGS I'LL NOT BE *TRIFLED* WITH.

WHAT *OBJECTION* CAN MY CAPTAIN-OF-GUARDS HAVE TO THAT?

A *GREAT* ONE...

IF YOU LET A FEW THOUSAND KUSHITES INTO YOUR PRECIOUS *INNER CITY--* THEN WORK UP THEIR BLOOD LUST BY WATCHING YOU SLAY ONE OF THEIR OWN-- IT WON'T TAKE MUCH TO SET OFF ANOTHER *UPRISING.*

I DO NOT *FEAR* THOSE BLACK SCUM!

MAYBE NOT. BUT I'VE SAVED YOUR PRETTY NECK FROM THEM *TWICE* ALREADY... AND THE THIRD TIME, MY LUCK MIGHT RUN OUT.

I'LL TAKE THAT CHANCE. NOW, GET *OUT* OF HERE!

I'VE WORK TO DO.

WITH YOUR LASH, YOU MEAN? AFARI TOLD ME *LORD TUTHMES* SENT YOU THIS CAPTIVE NEMEDIAN AS A SLAVE-- HE HAS *TASTE,* IF NOTHING ELSE.

AYE-- TASTE IN *SPIES,* FOR THAT'S WHY HE DOUBTLESS SENT HER TO ME.

I'LL SOON *FORCE* THE TRUTH OUT OF HER.

NOW, FOR THE FINAL TIME--*GET OUT!*

HAH! YOU'LL HAVE TO HURL YOUR WHIP-HANDLE HARDER THAN THAT TO HURT *MY* BACK, TANANDA.

COME, CHILD. WE'VE MUCH TO TALK ABOUT.

YOU-- *YOU*--!

OH, AND DON'T WORRY *TOO* MUCH ABOUT THE MASSES RISING AGAINST YOUR BENEVOLENT RULE, MY QUEEN.

CROM KNOWS, YOU DESERVE NO LESS... BUT I'LL POST MY *GUARDSMEN* CAREFULLY AT TONIGHT'S LITTLE BONFIRE.

I'M STILL BEING PAID TO *PROTECT* YOU, AND I KNOW MY JOB!

THEN, HIS LAUGH STILL RUMBLING BEHIND HIM, CONAN STRIDES OUT...

YOU SHALL *RUE* YOUR INSOLENCE, CONAN OF CIMMERIA!

SO SWEARS TANANDA, QUEEN OF KUSH!

MINUTES LATER, *SHUBBA*-- FAITHFUL RETAINER OF SCHEMING *LORD TUTHMES*-- PAUSES A MOMENT IN DRIVING A CHARIOT BACK TOWARD HIS MASTER'S HOUSE...

...AS HE IS ASTONISHED TO BEHOLD THE OUTLANDER CALLED *CONAN* CARRYING THE *NEMEDIAN SLAVE-WENCH* INTO HIS OWN QUARTERS.

MOVE, NAG!

MY LORD *TUTHMES* MUST KNOW OF THIS-- *AT ONCE!*

NIGHT COMES SOON TO *MEROÊ*, CAPITAL OF KUSH... BUT NOWHERE IS EITHER NIGHT OR PURPOSE DEEPER, DARKER, THAN IN THE CHAMBERS OF *LORD TUTHMES*, WHERE THAT WORTHY MEETS BOTH HIS MAN *SHUBBA*... AND WITH THE TALL KORDAFAN SORCERER, *MURU*.

HMMM... I SEE I DID NOT CREDIT QUEEN TANANDA WITH HER FULL MEASURE OF *SUSPICION*.

A PITY TO WASTE SO PROMISING AN INSTRUMENT AS THAT *NEMEDIAN GIRL*, BUT NOT EVERY SHAFT STRIKES THE MARK.

SO-- WHAT *NEXT*, I WONDER? HAS ANYONE SEEN OLD *AGEERA*, THE WITCH-SMELLER?

NAY, LORD TUTHMES. HE *VANISHED* AFTER STIRRING UP THAT RECENT RIOT AGAINST THE QUEEN.*

VERY *PRUDENTLY*, TOO, FOR HIS SAKE.

*LAST ISSUE. --ROY.

I THINK OUR FIRST ORDER OF BUSINESS SHOULD BE TO *GET RID* OF THAT GIRL, LEST SHE TELL *CONAN* WHAT LITTLE SHE KNOWS OF OUR PLOTTING.

MURU-- CAN YOU SEND YOUR *DEMON* TO CONAN'S QUARTERS WHILE HE'S COMMANDING HIS GUARDS-MEN TONIGHT-- TO *DO AWAY* WITH THE WENCH?

THAT I CAN, MASTER...

BUT, SHOULD I NOT COMMAND IT TO STAY THERE TILL CONAN RETURNS, AND SLAY *HIM*, TOO?

FOR, I SEE CLEARLY THAT YOU WILL *NEVER* BE KING, WHILE HE LIVES.

HE MAY HAVE COME TO MEROÊ AS A MERCENARY, BUT HE'S TOO *HONEST*, IN HIS WAY, TO BETRAY TANANDA LATER AND SERVE *OUR* CAUSE.

WELL ARGUED, WIZARD.

YES, LET US DISPOSE OF *BOTH* OF THEM AT THE SAME TIME!

I SHALL BE WATCHING THE *EXECUTION OF AAHMES* IN THE MAIN SQUARE, SO THAT NONE SHALL SAY I HAD A HAND IN THE SLAYINGS.

SOON, WHEN I'VE ALIGNED ENOUGH *NOBLES* BEHIND MY CAUSE, PER-HAPS I SHALL SET YOUR DEMON ON *TANANDA* AS WELL.

FOR NOW, I AM SATIS-FIED TO *WAIT*... MEANWHILE LETTING HER HANG HERSELF WITH HER OWN *EXCESSES*...!

Later-- ORNATE TORCHES ILLUMINATE AN INFERNAL SCENE IN THE MAIN SQUARE OF THE **INNER CITY,** THAT PART OF MEROË WHERE THE BROWN-SKINNED NOBILITY NORMALLY HIDE BEHIND THEIR **WALLS** FROM THE DARKER-SKINNED KUSHITES BEYOND.

TONIGHT, HOWEVER, THE DOORS TO THE INNER CITY HAVE BEEN OPENED-- AND ALL HAS BEEN ORDERLY THUS FAR.

INNOCENT, D-DO YOU HEAR M-ME??

NO-- PLEASE-- I **SWEAR** TO YOU, QUEEN TANANDA-- I AM **INNOCENT** OF TREASON!

BUT, WHO KNOWS WHAT WILL HAPPEN WHEN **PRIMITIVE PASSIONS** ARE STIRRED...

...AS STIRRED THEY SOON SHALL BE, BY THE MASKED **EXECUTIONER** WHO EVEN NOW STROKES THE TOOLS OF HIS GRISLY TRADE THROUGH A **FIRE** OF NEARLY WHITE HEAT.

131

NEARBY, THE SO-CALLED *NOBILITY* OF MEROË LOOK ON...

LORD AAHMES STILL PROCLAIMS HIS *INNOCENCE*, DOES HE-- AS IF IT WAS EVER REALLY IN *DOUBT!*

AYE, THE WAY I HEAR IT, THAT VERY INNOCENCE IN MATTERS OF POLITICS IS WHAT ENABLED *AFARI* TO TRAP AAHMES BY A *FALSE ACCUSATION.*

SHE'LL GO *TOO FAR* ONE DAY, OUR *TANANDA.*

I JUST HOPE SHE KNOWS WHAT SHE'S DOING, LETTING THE *OUTER CITY* IN TO WATCH...!

AT THAT OPPORTUNE MOMENT, *LORD TUTHMES* ARRIVES WITH HIS STRANGE ENTOURAGE.

FOR, EVEN A WOULD-BE *DESPOT* NEEDS AN AIRTIGHT *ALIBI* NOW AND THEN, DOES HE NOT?

AS FOR CONAN, HE HAS NO STOMACH FOR THE SIGHT NOW ABOUT TO ENFOLD BEFORE TANANDA'S IVORY THRONE.

HE CARES NOTHING FOR AAHMES HIMSELF, GUILTY OR NOT...

BUT, THIS IS NOT *HIS* WAY OF DEALING WITH ONE'S ENEMIES.

NOW HE BEHOLDS THE EXECUTIONER STALK TOWARD THE BOUND AND WIDE-EYED PRISONER...

NO-- NNOOO!

...AND KNOWS THAT HE IS DOUBTLESS ASKING AAHMES FOR DETAILS OF HIS ALLEGED *PLOT AGAINST THE THRONE.*

BUT, WHETHER AAHMES CONTINUES TO DENY, OR WHETHER HE CONFESSES TO CRIMES HE COULD NEVER HAVE COMMITTED...

...THE *END RESULT,* A FEW MINUTES HENCE, WILL BE THE SAME.

THEN, SUDDENLY, IT'S AS IF A *VOICE* IS SPEAKING INSIDE CONAN'S HEAD...

MONGO-- TAKE COMMAND TILL I RETURN!

YES, CAPTAIN CONAN.

IN THE HYBORIAN LANDS TO THE NORTH, CONAN HAS LISTENED TO THE SPECULATIONS OF *PRIESTS* AND *PHILOSOPHERS*.

THEY ARGUED OVER THE EXISTENCE OF *GUARDIAN SPIRITS*-- AND OVER THE POSSIBILITY OF *DIRECT COMMUNICATION* FROM MIND TO MIND.

BEING CONVINCED THEY WERE ALL *MAD*, CONAN DID NOT LISTEN... *AT THE TIME*.

NOW, HOWEVER, HE SUSPECTS SUDDENLY HE MAY JUST KNOW WHAT THEY *MEANT*.

THEN, EVEN AS HE DRAWS REIN IN FRONT OF HIS HOUSE--

AALEEE

D'ANA!

BY THE PRIVATES OF ISHTAR, I HEARD YOU *SCREAM*, GIRL.

NOW, WHERE THE DEVIL ARE--

BY THE BONES OF CROM!

AT THE DOOR OF THE LIVING ROOM, CONAN *HALTS*-- TRANSFIXED BY THE SCENE OF HORROR BEFORE HIM:

FOR, A *GRAY, COILING MIST* IS TAKING SHAPE AND FORM IN THE CENTER OF THE ROOM--

--A HULKING, *MONSTROUS* FORM WITH BRISTLING, PIG-LIKE SNOUT AND TUSKED, CHAMPING JAWS!

THE THING HAS SOLIDIFIED OUT OF THIN AIR, MATERIALIZING AS IF BY-- *MAGIC!*

AYE, *MAGIC*-- AND AS THE CREATURE STALKS TOWARD THE GIRL, *PRIMAL FEARS* RISE IN CONAN'S BARBARIAN MIND.

FOR HALF A HEARTBEAT, HIS SUPERSTITIONS MAKE HIM HESITATE. *THEN*--

CONAN! HELP ME-- IN MITRA'S NAME--!

I'M COMING, DIANA!

IN THE DARKNESS, HOWEVER, HE FAILS TO SEE THE FAINTED FORM OF HIS *FEMALE SERVANT*--

-- WITH DISASTROUS RESULTS!

OOOOOF--!

AT THE SELFSAME INSTANT, THE MONSTER *TURNS* WITH *SUPER-NATURAL* SWIFTNESS--

--TO *LAUNCH* ITSELF AT THE SPRAWLED CIMMERIAN IN A SINGLE HEADLONG *BOUND!*

RAWRR

AWNK

AWNK

CONAN'S PANTHERISH SPEED ENABLES HIM TO AVOID THE *FULL FORCE* OF THE THING'S HORRIFIC LEAP--

UNNH

--THOUGH EVEN *HE* CANNOT EVADE THE DEMON ENTIRELY--

AND, NEXT MOMENT, THOSE *GREAT CHISEL TUSKS* ARE THRUSTING *GLEAMING* FOR HIS THROAT!

NAY, HIS ENTIRE *HEAD* COULD VANISH WITHIN THOSE WIDE-GAPING JAWS.

YET, THOUGH CONAN IS PERHAPS THE MOST PHYSICALLY *POWERFUL* MAN OF HIS DAY AND AGE--

HRUNK

--SHEER STRENGTH IS NOT *ALL.*

A SECOND LATER, **BOTH** SNARLING COMBATANTS ARE ROLLING HEAD-ABOVE-HEELS UPON THE DEBRIS-LITTERED FLOOR--

--AND THE HAIRY CREATURE'S ARMS ENCIRCLE CONAN'S MASSIVE FORM WITH SUCH **CRUSHING FORCE** THAT A LESSER MAN'S BACK WOULD **SNAP** LIKE A ROTTED TWIG.

ARRRR!

GRARRR

RRRRI

THE GROWLS MADE BY THE TWO ARE NOT MUCH DIFFERENT, EACH FROM EACH.

THE **WEIGHT** OF THE TWO, LIKEWISE, IS NEARLY THE SAME...

GRONXX

BUT THE DEMON'S SHEER, RAW STRENGTH IS **INCREDIBLE**...

...AND HARDLY TO BE RECKONED IN HUMAN TERMS!

:UNNGHN--!:

THEN, EVEN AS HE **STRAINS** HIS EVERY MUSCLE TO THE UTMOST--

-- THE CIMMERIAN FEELS HIS **FOREARM** BEING BENT SLOWLY, RE-LENTLESSLY BACK--

--SEES THE **SNOUTED JAWS** COME CLOSER, **CLOSER** TO HIS FACE!

ONLY A DESPERATE *WRITHING* AT THE LAST MOMENT SAVES HIM LONG ENOUGH TO CRY OUT--

DIANA! MY SWORD!

IN CROM'S NAME-- TOSS ME MY *SWORD!*

BUT, THE NEMEDIAN SLAVE-GIRL STANDS STARK STILL, RIVETED WITH THE *HORROR* OF THE SCENE--

AND IT IS ONLY WHEN SHE SENSES THAT HER WOULD-BE RESCUER HAS GIVEN HIS *ALL* IN ONE FINAL, SOULWRENCHING *PUSH--*

:MMMFF!:

HRONK

:HUHNNNGH--:

--THRUSTING OUT A BRONZED AND CLUTCHING HAND THAT FALLS *JUST SHORT* OF ITS METALLICALLY-GLEAMING GOAL--

--THAT SHE IS SUDDENLY GALVANIZED INTO *ACTION--*

HERE, CONAN-- *HERE!*

THERE IS SCANT TIME FOR CONAN TO TEST FOR A *SOFT SPOT* IN THE MONSTER'S LEATHERY HIDE--

--ONLY TO *THRUST,* AND BE GLAD WHEN THE BLADE BITES *DEEP--*

AWKKK

--AND TO **LEAP FREE** WITH A GASPING INTAKE OF BREATH, WHEN THE THING RELAXES ITS GRIP FOR A FLEETING SECOND!

GRONK

CONAN! YOU DID IT!

NOT *YET,* GIRL! THAT DEVIL'S STILL *ALIVE*--

--AND MY STRENGTH'S *EBBING,* MOMENT BY MOMENT.

ONLY ONE WAY TO KEEP IT FROM *CLOSING* WITH ME AGAIN--!

ONLY ONE WAY!

BOTH HANDS ON HIS SWORD-HILT NOW, CONAN SWINGS HIS BLADE IN A FLASHING, DESPERATE *ARC*--

--AND SENDS THE CREATURE STAGGERING BACKWARD, ITS HEAD HALF SEVERED BY THE MIGHTY STROKE!

AWNK

A HEARTBEAT MORE, AND THE DEMON HAS CRASHED LOUDLY TO THE FLOOR...

I-- I'M SO *GLAD*--

I PRAYED TO *ISHTAR*-- TO SEND YOU--!

WHOA, GIRL. TAKE IT EASY. I'M *HERE*... I CAME...

AND I MAY *LOOK* READY FOR THE GRAVE, BUT I CAN STILL *STAND,* SO--

WHAT IN *HELL'S THOUSAND* NAMES--?

WH-WHAT IS IT, CONAN? I-I'M AFRAID TO LOOK...!

THE *DEMON*-- IT'S STILL *ALIVE*--AND IT'S STAGGERED OUT INTO THE NIGHT!

PLEASE, CONAN-- DON'T *FOLLOW* IT! WE MUST--

LATER, GIRL, FOR *CROM'S* SAKE!

THAT'S THE *DEMON OF THE NIGHT* THEY TALK ABOUT--

AND, BY YMIR, I MEAN TO FIND OUT WHERE IT *COMES FROM!*

GONE, DAMN ITS LEATHER HIDE-- AND IT'S FRIGHTENED OFF MY HORSE, TO BOOT!

BUT, THEY SAY A MORTALLY WOUNDED DEMON-THING WILL ALWAYS SEEK OUT ITS *HUMAN MASTER*--

--SO I'M BETTING I KNOW WHERE IT'S CRAWLED OFF TO *DIE!*

IN THE MAIN SQUARE OF THE INNER CITY, THE PITIFUL THING THAT ONCE WAS LORD AAHMES HAS BEEN *SLOWER* TO DIE THAN ONE WOULD HAVE THOUGHT.

YET, DIE HE *HAS,* AT LAST, JUST IN TIME FOR...

AIEEE! WHAT IS *THAT?*

IT'S THE *DEMON!*

THE *DEMON OF THE NIGHT!*

AYE, THE MAN SPEAKS TRUTH! IT'S THE *DEVIL* THAT HAS PLAGUED US FOR YEARS--

BUT, IT SEEMS *WOUNDED UNTO DEATH!*

THEN *WHY* DOES IT STAGGER TOWARD--

--MURU, THE KORDAFAN!?

THE ANSWER, AFTER A BRIEF HUSH, IS NOT LONG IN COMING--

SLAY HIM! HE IS THE DEMON'S MASTER!

YES-- *KILL HIM!*

KILL HIM!

CONAN HAS REACHED THE SQUARE ON FOOT BY NOW, AND HAS BEEN ON THE VERGE OF PLUNGING INTO THE CROWD, TO FINISH OFF THE MONSTER... IF FINISHING OFF IS WHAT IT NEEDS.

HE QUICKLY THINKS *BETTER* OF THE IDEA.

SLAY THE WIZARD FROM KORDAFA!

HE'S ALREADY *DEAD* -- CAN'T YOU *SEE?*

LOOK! THERE'S OLD *AGEERA,* THE WITCH-SMELLER-- COME OUT OF *HIDING* AT LAST!

MEN OF MEROÊ-- WHY SLAY THE *TOOL,* AND NOT THE MAN WHO *WIELDS* IT?

THERE STANDS HE WHOM THE KORDAFAN *SERVED.*

AT HIS COMMAND, THE DEMON SLEW *AMBOOLA* -- SO MY SPIRITS HAVE TOLD ME IN THE SILENCE OF THE TEMPLE OF JULLA!

SLAY HIM--

--SLAY *TUTHMES,* TRUE MASTER OF THE NIGHT-DEMON!

NO! NNOOOOO

TUTHMES' CRIES ARE *LOUD,* IF NOT LONG-LIVED.

NOR IS AGEERA FINISHED...

SLAY *ALL* THE LORDS! CAST OFF YOUR BONDS! *KILL YOUR MASTERS!*

KILL! KILL! KILL!

AND, AS THE BLACKS OF MEROÉ RESPOND RABIDLY TO THE WITCH-SMELLER'S SHRIEKS--

--CONAN RECALLS THAT THE MEN WHO *GUARD* KUSH'S DUSKY QUEEN... ARE *BLACK.*

QUEEN TANANDA, ALAS, DOES NOT.

GUARDS! KILL THOSE BLACK DOGS -- STARTING WITH THAT DAMNED *PRIEST!*

DO YOU HEAR ME? *KILL THEM!*

THE GUARDSMAN CLOSEST TO THE ROYAL PERSONAGE DOES NOT SPEAK IN ANSWER...

BUT, HIS RESPONSE BESPEAKS CENTURIES OF *REPRESSION* BY THE DUSKY-SKINNED ONES OF THE BLACK POPULACE.

WHO CAN SAY *WHAT* MAKES MEN ACT THUS, SUDDENLY, AFTER LONG YEARS OF SERVITUDE AND BETRAYAL OF THEIR OWN KIND?

EEEGK

ONLY *ACTIONS* CAN BE SEEN, NOT THOUGHTS...

...AND ACTIONS *BEGET* ACTIONS--

THE QUEEN IS DEAD! KILL ALL THE LORDS OF MEROÉ!

BE *FREE MEN* AGAIN-- AND NOT *SLAVES!*

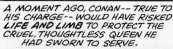

A MOMENT AGO, CONAN-- TRUE TO HIS CHARGE-- WOULD HAVE RISKED **LIFE AND LIMB** TO PROTECT THE CRUEL, THOUGHTLESS QUEEN HE HAD SWORN TO SERVE.

THAT'S THE WAY HE IS.

NO USE, HOWEVER, IN PROTECTING A CORPSE.

BESIDES, CONAN IS BRONZE OF SKIN, FOR ALL HIS YEARS SOUTH OF STYGIA.

HE DOESN'T FOOL HIMSELF INTO BELIEVING HE COULD JOIN THE REBELLION... OR EVEN **SURVIVE** IT FOR LONG.

DIANA! LET'S GO-- AND DON'T DROP THAT **LOAF** OF BREAD!

I'M **COMING**-- BUT, WHAT OF THE **WEALTH** THAT'S--

WE'VE GOT OUR **LIVES**, GIRL--

LET'S NOT **PRESS** OUR LUCK!

ALREADY AS THEY FLEE, MEROÉ'S INNER CITY IS ABLAZE WITH YELLOW PYRAMIDS OF FLAME.

OVERHEAD, LIGHTNING FLASHES, AS IF ON CUE...

...AND IT IS RAINING BY THE TIME THEY'VE REACHED OPEN COUNTRY.

CROM! THE PEOPLE OF THE DARK KINGDOMS ARE AS THICK-HEADED AS MY **OWN** TRIBESMEN.

I SWEAR I'LL ALMOST BE GLAD TO BE BACK IN THE **HYBORIAN LANDS** AGAIN.

AND WHAT OF **YOU**, GIRL?...

I'LL SEND YOU HOME TO NEMEDIA, OR KEEP YOU **WITH** ME... WHICHEVER YOU PREFER.

I THINK... IN SPITE OF THE **WET** AND ALL...

...I LIKE THINGS...AS THEY **ARE**...!

CONAN GRINS SILENTLY IN THE FIRE-SHOT DARKNESS, AND URGES HIS HORSE TO A TROT.

NEXT: MAN-EATERS of DARFAR!

"... countless malformed limbs and appendages and heads ..."

A Few Personal Notes on
Conan the Barbarian #92,101–107
by Roy Thomas

So after Bêlit died and Conan burned her body on her ship, *The Tigress* . . .

But, I'm getting a bit ahead of myself.

Before I start talking about the story from Marvel's **Conan the Barbarian** #101, I need to say a few words about an earlier issue, one that Dark Horse had to skip in the previous volume of this **Chronicles of Conan** series.

CtB #92's "The Thing in the Crypt" was what we call in the field a "fill-in" issue, which had interrupted, for one month, the flow of events in Conan's drive to put Bêlit back on the throne of her native city Asgalun, in Shem. It was pencilled by Sal Buscema, younger brother of regular **CtB** artist John Buscema, and inked by regular embellisher Ernie Chan . . . and was based on a prose tale by L. Sprague de Camp and Lin Carter which had seen print nearly a decade earlier. The note on the splash page of #92 says it was tossed in because John was on vacation in France and Italy, and that's probably true . . . although I suspect I had given Sal this particular story some time earlier, with the idea that it'd be printed sooner or later, either in **CtB** or in its black-&-white companion magazine **The Savage Sword of Conan.**

"Crypt" relates a single eventful night very, very early in the Cimmerian's colorful career—when he was in his late teens and hadn't yet journeyed to Southern Hyboria. De Camp and Carter had told how Conan had been captured by and escaped from the hated Hyperboreans in the frozen North, and soon acquired a sword from a giant skeleton in a subterranean tomb. It was a slight enough story, but it was full of fast-paced action and I rather liked it. (Before Marvel had acquired the rights to adapt de Camp's additions to the Conan canon, I had plotted a parallel tale as a flashback in **CtB** #31—see Vol. 5 of this series—and the two adventures were just similar enough that it took a convoluted bit of explaining at the end of #92 to reconcile the two issues.)

With that out of the way, we move on to **Conan the Barbarian** #101 and points beyond.

The accepted (and logical) timeline for the hero, following Bêlit's tragic death in issue #100, called for him to cut north overland through the Black Kingdoms, headed for the so-called "civilized" nations. Since, starting with #1 back in 1970, I had always had approximately a year of real time pass in Conan's life for each year's worth of **CtB** issues, I had to allow a number of issues (which equalled months) to take place in the Hyborian Age's equivalent of equatorial Africa. After all, the Cimmerian was no superhero who could go flying up to Nemedia or Zingara.

"The Devil Has Many Legs" is the potboiler of a story I came up with first. And as I look back at it, I don't think it's half bad—or at least, John Buscema and Ernie Chan made it look good with their artistic rendering of it. We'd done giant spiders before, but it had been a while. You know how it is with sword and sorcery—every so often, you just *have* to throw a giant spider into a story. It's in the contract somewhere. And I relished a chance to show that the Black Kingdoms, which Robert E. Howard rarely visited in his stories, could be just as interesting as Aquilonia or Zamora.

Someone did write in a letter about the splash page of #101 that I still recall after all these years. The missive-maven found humor in the fact that the story opened with Conan sitting around roasting a big hunk of meat over a fire, and muttering to himself, "Bêlit . . ." To that particular reader, the juxtaposition made it look as if it were the thigh-bone of the late Queen of the Black Coast that the Cimmerian was heating up. Weird, these comics fans.

Issue #102's "The Men Who Drink Blood" was even more fun, with the locals' sanguinary notion of liquid refreshment. Actually, the springboard for the idea was my knowledge that the Masai of East Africa did indeed imbibe the blood of ritually slaughtered cattle (though I wouldn't see the Masai or their country close up till 1994). I simply turned them into a sort of "living vampire"—a term I'd used several years earlier for my co-creation Morbius in **The Amazing Spider-Man** #101—and ran with it. I got two issues out of the story line, actually, including #103's "Bride of the Vampire."

(I must've been in a mood to work the epithets of comic book characters into dialogue around that time. Besides the "living vampire" bit, in #102 I have Conan call the Bamula "brothers of the spear"—the name of a long-running series in the back of Dell's **Tarzan** comics of the 1950s, originally drawn by the young but already fine artist Russ Manning. I always meant little touches like that to be an additional kick for the older and more knowledgeable fan, while not distracting for the younger or more casual reader for whom that issue of **Conan the Barbarian** might be his very first comic book.)

After those three original stories, I got a chance in #104 to adapt another REH story: "The Vale of Lost Women." This was not one of Howard's best—in fact, not a few of his admirers consider it the *worst* Conan story he ever wrote. Some editor somewhere may have agreed; the tale wasn't published until three decades following the author's suicide in 1936. Still, it *was* a Howard Conan story, so I was bound and determined to adapt it—and it really didn't make a bad comic book issue.

Two things commend this story to my memory. One is the fact that it contains the only mention ever by Howard of "Kheshatta, City of Magicians," a mysterious locale in Stygia. The phrase always fascinated me—as it doubtless did some-time Conan prose writer Lin Carter, who in the late 1960s had scribed a paperback novel titled **Thongor and the City of Magicians**—and I wondered what a city with a sobriquet like that might possibly be like! After all, it's not as if the rest of Stygia was exactly lacking in the black magic department—so a whole "City of Magicians" must really be something to see! Alas, Howard gives no clue—for the story's heroine Livia is captured by the savage Bakalah en route to the place, and never gets there! (It was thus left to me to set a multi-part tale in Kheshatta when I became scripter of **The Savage Sword of Conan** again in the 1990s—and it was one of my favorite story arcs.)

The other thing I loved about "The Vale of Lost Women" was a line of dialogue Conan speaks near the end of the story. After killing the "demon from the dark" that tries to fly off with Livia, he casually dismisses the creature as just one of many: "They're thick as fleas outside the belt of light that surrounds this world." Howard had a real way with a phrase, and this disparagement by Conan of the fanged, bat-winged monstrosity he's just slain strikes precisely the right note.

Issue #105, too, was an adaptation, this time of a story by de Camp and Carter. The original title of the tale on which "Whispering Shadows" is based was "Castle of Terror." But the Comics Code to which all Marvel's comic books had to conform had a hard and fast rule, and had since the mid-1950s: the words "horror" and "terror" could not be used on a comic book cover, or in the title of a comic book story. Well, this is one time I didn't mind making a change to satisfy the code. "Castle of Terror" was a strictly generic title—not that "Whispering Shadows" was all that much better, I suppose.

The tricky part of this adaptation was the appearance of the monster which takes form from the shadows while the slavers sleep. It's all very well to describe a creature composed of "countless malformed limbs and appendages and heads"—quite another thing to *draw* the darn thing so it looks frightening rather than faintly ridiculous. It's the same problem artists in both comics and movies have had when trying to visualize the alien in John W. Campbell's classic science-fiction horror story "Who Goes There?" Still, John Buscema pulled it off, even if it wasn't a page he'd have stuck in his sample portfolio. The monster doesn't appear in many panels, anyway—it's just there to mop up the slave-masters. Atypically, Conan doesn't even fight the blasted thing—he just kills a fear-maddened Stygian who attacks him, steals a horse, and heads north again. Probably the best thing to do, under the circumstances.

And then came "The Snout in the Dark," in **Conan the Barbarian** #106-107.

I've always felt bad that somehow, on the splash page of #106, I managed to give credit for the story to de Camp and Carter, "featuring the epic hero created by Robert E. Howard." Because, actually, the germ of the story and several pages of the prose version were Howard's, and actually all three writers duly shared credit on the prose version. (I'm glad to say I got the byline right in the second part.)

The part of the story adapted from words written by REH begins on the second page of "Chaos in the Land Called Kush," where Amboola, chained in a dungeon, is slain by a materializing demon with a piglike snout; it runs through the thirteenth page (plus the events of the final two panels on the fourteenth). The remainder of that issue and all of the next is mostly de Camp and Carter . . . and the admixture actually makes for a reasonably exciting tale, I think. REH's two "posthumous collaborators" threw in a whipping scene out of "Xuthal of the Dusk" and **Red Nails**, a bit of palace intrigue by way of several other stories, and of course the climactic battle with the ol' snout-monster itself, which John and I milked for several pages.

One-time Marvel editor-in-chief Tom De Falco—maybe quoting Stan Lee—has said that in a Marvel comic, "the fight" is often the least important or interesting thing. Somehow, though, I never quite saw it that way. Whether it was the battle between young Conan and the Man-Serpent back in **CtB #7**, which Barry Smith and I had verbally choreographed in a London hotel lobby one summer night in 1970, or the four-page free-for-all in **CtB #107** which John pretty much designed from de Camp and Carter's description, I relished those struggles. Perhaps it's because, unlike the superhero combats in most Marvel mags, I was a believer—especially in the Conan comics—in writing dramatic captions to underscore the action. So it wasn't just "Pow!" "Slam!" and a couple of wisecracks.

Much of the wording on those four nigh-dialogue-less pages, of course, is an adaptation of the work of de Camp and Carter—but I tossed in a bit of my own, as well, in order to make the actions flow and to give them added meaning. This is an area where my artist friend Gil Kane and I and a few others disagreed with the usual "less is more" doctrine. To Gil and me, those words added emotions and tension and texture that a few pages' worth of pictures alone, even if they were very *good* pictures, could not convey by themselves.

For example, at the top of the eleventh page of "Demon of the Night," panel 2, the caption says that the snout-thing's arms encircle Conan "with such crushing force that a lesser man's back would snap like a rotted twig." The picture, as pencilled by Buscema and inked by Chan, conveys a certain amount of that strength and ferocity—but the quoted words quantify the beast-thing's power. Without checking, I'm not sure if that phrase is from de Camp and Carter's story, or if I added it. I suspect the latter, but it makes no difference. I'm not indifferent by any means to the virtues of occasionally letting a sequence stand with no words whatsoever . . . but, to me, this wasn't one of those places where that was the better course.

Hmm . . . now that I look back over the eight issues of **Conan the Barbarian** re-presented in this volume, I see that they are the work of no less than three artists—and four writers, counting those whose work was adapted. To me, that was one of the fun things about writing that series. It offered me a chance to make up stories of my own whenever I wanted to . . . or to adapt the words and mental pictures of the man who had created Conan . . . or to play around with the notions and phrasing of other talented writers, as well.

Is it any wonder that I stuck around for ten years—and indeed would leave **Conan the Barbarian** only when I left Marvel itself, some months later?

But, at this time, I wasn't thinking at all about leaving Marvel, or **Conan**. I was just putting the Cimmerian through his pugnacious paces—and as far as I was concerned, I was prepared to go on writing his epic adventures forever . . .

Roy Thomas wrote every issue of Marvel's *Conan the Barbarian*, *Savage Sword of Conan*, and *King Conan* from 1970 through 1980, then again from circa 1990 until Marvel relinquished the franchise at the end of that decade. He also co-scripted the second Arnold Schwarzenegger movie, *Conan the Destroyer*, and has written the swashbuckling Cimmerian in several other media, as well.